T0339551

Cambridge Elements ≡

Elements in Global Urban History
edited by
Michael Goebel
Graduate Institute Geneva
Tracy Neumann
Wayne State University
Joseph Ben Prestel
Freie Universität Berlin

THE MODERN CITY IN ASIA

Kristin Stapleton
University at Buffalo

Shaftesbury Road, Cambridge CB2 8EA, United Kingdom

One Liberty Plaza, 20th Floor, New York, NY 10006, USA

477 Williamstown Road, Port Melbourne, VIC 3207, Australia

314–321, 3rd Floor, Plot 3, Splendor Forum, Jasola District Centre, New Delhi – 110025, India

103 Penang Road, #05–06/07, Visioncrest Commercial, Singapore 238467

Cambridge University Press is part of Cambridge University Press & Assessment, a department of the University of Cambridge.

We share the University's mission to contribute to society through the pursuit of education, learning and research at the highest international levels of excellence.

www.cambridge.org
Information on this title: www.cambridge.org/9781108994927
DOI: 10.1017/9781108992947

© Kristin Stapleton 2022

This publication is in copyright. Subject to statutory exception and to the provisions of relevant collective licensing agreements, no reproduction of any part may take place without the written permission of Cambridge University Press & Assessment.

First published 2022

A catalogue record for this publication is available from the British Library.

ISBN 978-1-108-99492-7 Paperback
ISSN 2632-3192 (print)
ISSN 2632-3206 (online)

Cambridge University Press & Assessment has no responsibility for the persistence or accuracy of URLs for external or third-party internet websites referred to in this publication and does not guarantee that any content on such websites is, or will remain, accurate or appropriate.

The Modern City in Asia

Elements in Global Urban History

DOI: 10.1017/9781108992947
First published online: May 2022

Kristin Stapleton
University at Buffalo

Author for correspondence: Kristin Stapleton, kstaple@buffalo.edu

Abstract: Kristin Stapleton analyzes how concepts and practices associated with the "modern city" were received, transformed, and contested in Asia over the past 150 years. In the early twentieth century, activists took advantage of the new significance of the city to pursue a wide variety of goals. Thus, the concept of the modern city played an important role in Asia, despite much critical commentary on the ideals associated with it. By the 1940s, the city yielded its political centrality to the nation. Still, modern cities remained an important marker of national achievement during the Cold War. In recent decades, cities have continued to play a central role in economic and cultural affairs in Asia, but the concept of the modern city has evolved. Asian ideas about urban governance and visions of future cities are significantly shaping that evolution.

Keywords: Asia, cities, governance, history, urbanization

© Kristin Stapleton 2022

ISBNs: 9781108994927 (PB), 9781108992947 (OC)
ISSNs: 2632-3206 (online), 2632-3192 (print)

Contents

1 Introduction: Asia's Urban History and the Concept of the Modern City

Throughout much of human history, the largest, wealthiest, and most technologically advanced cities in the world could be found in Asia. Asian cities have taken many shapes over the centuries, including as centers of administration, pilgrimage, and trade. Cities were integrated in various ways into broader polities and economic networks. Poets, historians, and travel writers celebrated their respective attractions. Political theorists and philosophers incorporated the phenomenon of cities into governance frameworks and idealizations of locality, world, and universe that evolved over time.

Beginning two centuries ago, Asian communities encountered a new and powerful conception of cities that had developed primarily in the context of Western Europe's industrialization and then spread around the world. The emergence of the concept of the "modern city" resulted from worldwide developments in the early modern period. In the decades around 1900, though, the modern city was presented by its advocates as a special cultural product of a putative "Western civilization." European, American, and Japanese imperialism promoted the spread of the new ideas about cities and urban governance in those decades, but new communication networks also allowed Asian activists to access such information outside of the direct control of imperialist authorities. Both "modern" and "city" being notoriously hard to define, what exactly constituted the modern city was always debated; nevertheless, as we shall see, it was a powerful concept linked to awe-inspiring technologies that transformed social and political life. In her study of Japanese "urban-centrism" in the 1920s and 1930s, Louise Young (2013: 18) writes that "the idea that modern cities possessed a kind of manifest destiny to expand their territory, power, and resources" was common in Japan and throughout the world during those decades. Alternative visions arose from within and beyond Asia to challenge urban-centrism to some effect, but, particularly in postcolonial Asian states, new governments often adopted development policies that perpetuated it.

This Element examines how the new conception of the modern city was received and contested, actualized, and transformed in various parts of Asia over time, focusing primarily on the past 150 years. I argue that this period witnessed both an unprecedented obsession with cities and the growth of city-centered politics in Asia. During the decades before and after 1900, entrepreneurs and activists took advantage of the new significance of the city as an economic engine, cultural center, and site of governance to pursue a wide variety of goals. Thus, the concept of the modern city played an important role in Asia during a tumultuous era, despite much critical commentary on the ideals associated with it. By the 1940s, the city yielded its political centrality to the nation, as decolonization efforts gained ground and new nations emerged from the ashes of WWII. Still, modern cities remained an important marker of national achievement during the Cold War. In recent decades, cities have continued to play a central role in economic and cultural affairs in Asia, but the concept of the modern city has transformed markedly, a process that continues today. Asian ideas about urban governance and visions of future cities are significantly shaping that transformation.

As is the case with cities throughout the world, ordinary people did almost all the work of building and maintaining Asia's cities, in addition to shaping their cultures in many ways. This Element focuses primarily on how cities were conceptualized among elites who claimed authority over them or who led movements critical of them. As a result, the experiences of the majority of cities' inhabitants are but lightly touched on. It is to be hoped that future contributions to this series will spotlight popular conceptions of the city and daily life in modern Asian cities.

1.1 The Nineteenth-Century Concept of the Modern City

In the late nineteenth century, writes historian Daniel Rodgers (1998: 212), "the city stood at the vital center of transatlantic progressive imaginations." In Western Europe and the United States, industrialization had led to rapid urbanization and increasing concern about disease, poor housing conditions, social fragmentation, and crime. In addition to jeopardizing human health and safety, industrialization enriched cities. Wealth concentrated in the hands of a minority, but city governments gradually learned how to pry some of it out of those hands to improve the urban environment for a broader public. Industrialists and merchants appreciated the benefits of better transportation infrastructure to facilitate the movement of goods, and municipal governments gained the authority to manage improvements in that area. Health crises, property crime, and labor unrest led to new experiments in municipal policing and sanitation. Gradually, municipal governments took on more and more urban services, with activists calling for the municipal provision of water, gas, electricity, schools, and hospitals and for traffic control and enforcement of regulations on buildings and commerce. Activists outside government pressured the officials and merchants to improve urban conditions and organized associations to promote reforms and offer public services.

Technological marvels – steam-powered factories, gas illumination, and steel-framed multistoried buildings – revolutionized urban life. Simultaneously, the money and goods flowing through cities created a fertile environment for public culture. Newspapers and social clubs proliferated. Museums and public gardens and music halls appeared. Entrepreneurial innovation nourished a new urban consumer culture that almost everyone could participate in to some extent.

The industrializing cities of Western Europe and North America, with their expanding municipal administrations and associational life, engaged in intercity competition to earn recognition as culturally advanced and well managed – considered key criteria for being "modern," that amorphous but desirable quality. They also inspired the formulation of a body of social theory about the role of cities in human history. Historians pointed to the emergence of "burgher" (German for "merchant") society in late medieval European cities as the beginning of the end of the feudal era. Burghers, also known as the bourgeoisie, demanded urban self-rule, complete with a legal system that protected property rights. Thus, liberal theorists saw cities as the source of civilization: the cradle of the Enlightenment, where ancient Greek democratic values had been revived and could best grow. More radical thinkers, such as Karl Marx, conceived of cities – the headquarters of the bourgeoisie – as sites of class struggle, where workers would one day seize power from their capitalist exploiters.

Regardless of ideological bent, late nineteenth-century European and American social theorists and activists fixated on technologically advanced, firmly regulated cities as centers of change and progress. This is the conception of the modern city that made its way around the world in the decades before and after 1900. Modern cities were thought to reflect the great achievements of progressive "Western civilization." Writing in the early twentieth century and without having set foot in Asia, sociologist Max Weber provided a sophisticated theoretical framework to support the judgment that Asian cities lacked the rational organization and progressive dynamism commonly associated with modern cities (Rowe 1984; Sunar 2019).

Thus, many European and Americans of the time thought of their own cities as distinctive. They were modern, while cities in the rest of the world were not. In the seventeenth and eighteenth centuries, European travelers had been impressed by the size and wealth of many Asian cities. In the nineteenth century, though, reports tended to stress disorder, lethargy, and squalor as defining characteristics of Asian cities. Nineteenth-century travel accounts published in English often note that Asian cities seemed like "big villages." By then, many of the port cities of South and Southeast Asia had been taken over or destroyed by imperialist European expansion, and the two great East and South Asian empires, the Qing and the Mughal, were in decline for a whole host of reasons. More important than indigenous Asian developments for understanding the power of the concept of the modern city, though, was the growth of Western

European economic and political dominance, which gave the concept a cultural authority that made it both highly attractive and difficult to dispute (although, as we shall see, some prominent Asian activists did challenge it). In the history of the concept of the modern city in Asia, we can trace the rise and fall of a world view.

1.2 Why Asia? What Asia?

The modern city concept circled the globe in the decades around 1900. A global history of its reception and transformation could and ought to be written, but to do so within the constraints of a Cambridge Element would be a difficult challenge. Globalized history has become a popular genre before most Anglophone readers have been able to acquire even rudimentary familiarity with local histories in much of the world and gain appreciation of the rich texture of community life outside of Western Europe and the United States.

The writer Pankaj Mishra, while not focused on cities, illustrates the value of highlighting the human scale in world history. In *From the Ruins of Empire: The Revolt Against the West and the Remaking of Asia* (2012), he shows how prominent Asian thinkers – including Jamal al-Din al-Afghani, Liang Qichao, and Rabindranath Tagore – reformulated local cultural knowledge and helped other Asians imagine how to challenge Euro-American conceptual frameworks in the twentieth century. Mishra's "Asia" includes the areas encompassed by the Qing, Mughal, and Ottoman empires. This Element adopts a more compact geographical conception of Asia, extending from Japan and Korea in the east, through Southeast Asia and China, to the territory of British India (today's Bangladesh, India, and Pakistan).

Like any attempt to divide the world up for analytical purposes, this Japan-to-Pakistan conception of Asia has its limitations. As Lewis and Wigen (1997: 194) point out in their call for "more supple and sophisticated frameworks" to capture "the plasticity of spatial forms and the plurality of spatial identities," all analytical efforts to slice and dice the world are political. The geographical framework of this Element has been shaped by the history of area studies in the United States – my own academic training was done within the institutional environment established there in the wake of WWII, when the Association for Asian Studies claimed a mandate to promote knowledge of what came to be called East, Southeast, and South Asia while paying some attention to Central Asia. Although there were many obvious strong connections over the centuries between South Asia, Southwest Asia (the Middle East), and Eastern and Northern Africa, they have been de-emphasized within Asian studies scholarly communities until recently. The rise of the concept of the Global South (see Section 6.2) is gradually changing that older area studies perspective, and no doubt more comparative urban histories will adopt that framework in the future (Parnell and Oldfield 2014).

Despite the limitations of this Element's geographic framework, I do want to emphasize how enjoyable and enlightening it has been to widen my own China-focused urban history expertise and bring it into conversation with the work of specialists in contiguous regions. Scholars such as Ananya Roy and Aihwa Ong have noted the usefulness of working within the framework of Asia even in the absence of a clear definition (Roy and Ong 2011: preface; see also Chen and Chua 2007). Citing Gayatri Spivak's *Other Asias*, Jini Kim Watson (2011: 254) notes that "the loose signifier of 'Asia' . . . holds potential as both a regionalizing and pluralizing concept that will undo the bilateralism between the West and the non-West." I hope that my efforts along these lines will stimulate comparison and critique among urban historians with expertise in other areas of the world – particularly in other parts of Asia and in Africa and Latin America.

As this Element will show, the aspiration to build modern cities and the imperative to critique them brought Asian people together across national borders. Colonial cities such as Hong Kong, Singapore, and Bombay impressed Chinese and Japanese observers in the nineteenth century. In the twentieth century, Mohandas K. Gandhi and Mao Zedong attracted followers across Asia and beyond as they attacked the dominance of the modern city concept and articulated alternative visions of social progress. In the twenty-first century, Asian organizations and activists are increasingly shaping the global conversation about cities.

2 Colonial Cities in the Age of European Imperialism

Ports constructed in many Asian harbors link the land and the sea in what historians call the Indian Ocean world. Janet Abu-Lughod (1991) traces the flourishing of commerce across that world that coincided with the rise and decline of the Mongol empire. By the late seventeenth century, two powerful empires, the Qing and the Mughal, had claimed control of huge expanses of continental Asia, and the booming economies they presided over stimulated trade even more. Their political capitals, Beijing and Delhi, did not themselves face the sea, but commercial entrepôts proliferated within and outside their territory, on the coasts of the Indian Ocean and the South China Sea.

Some of these port cities had very long histories, while others were more ephemeral. Guangzhou in southern China supplied porcelain, silk, and tea to the rest of maritime Asia for more than 1,500 years (Fong 2014). Artisans produced jewelry and other goods in Cambay in the northwestern Indian region of Gujarat, a center for trade with the Arab and Persian worlds from around 1000 CE until its decline in the seventeenth century. Chittagong in the Bay of Bengal and Masulipatnam on the Coromandel coast connected producers and consumers in those regions with their counterparts in Southeast Asia and beyond (Ray 2017). The communities that constituted port cities were constantly in flux, given the contingencies of trade and environmental constraints in the age of sail. In much of maritime Southeast Asia, port cities grew and declined rapidly, as harbors silted up and the political environment grew more or less welcoming (Blussé 2013).

In the sixteenth century, the Portuguese entered the Indian Ocean world, followed by the Spanish, Dutch, British, and French. Sophisticated ships and weaponry supported their ambitions to dominate trade and spread Christianity. A new chapter in Asian urban history opened as European powers established fortresses and then urban bases in the west and south of India and across Southeast Asia. By the nineteenth century, the British, Dutch, Spanish, and French controlled expansive colonies: British India and Malaya, the Netherlands East Indies, the Spanish Philippines, and French Indochina. In the second half of the nineteenth century, the modern city concept was introduced in colonial capitals and spread within a context of political and economic inequality and racism. Still, many people in Asia found the concept useful for their own purposes.

2.1 Asian Port Cities and European Adventurers

The great transformation European colonization wrought in the relationship between cities and the wider world of maritime Asia is clearly illustrated in the history of the Straits of Malacca (the Straits). That waterway offered the easiest route between India and China (see Map 1). Its dominant city before the 1500s was Melaka. The city emerged around 1400 in the wake of the collapse of Srivijaya, a maritime empire that had dominated the region from its base in Sumatra. As documented by ShawnaKim Lowey-Ball (2015), the rulers of Melaka, who claimed descent from the Srivijaya royal family, made its port the center of intra-Asian trade with their openness to foreign people and ideas.

Admiral Zheng He's Ming treasure ships regularly awaited the changing of the monsoon winds in Melaka's port beginning in 1407. Melaka's second ruler adopted the Muslim title of sultan and encouraged Muslim traders and clerics to take up residence, although he may not himself have been a believer. Lowey-Ball argues that pre-1500 Melaka flourished as no Asian city-state had before, thanks to its growing multiethnic bureaucracy, tolerance for cultural diversity,

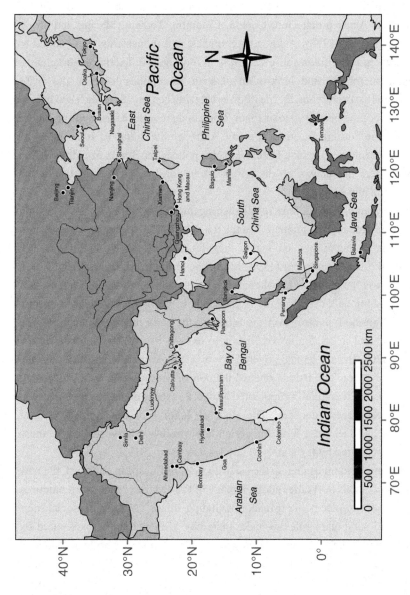

Map 1 Asian cities mentioned in Sections 2–4. Map designed by Collin O'Connor, Department of Geography, University at Buffalo, SUNY

legal code to regulate conduct among strangers, and singular focus on trade. By 1500, some 150,000 people lived there. In 1511, however, the Portuguese conquest brought the Melaka experiment to an abrupt end.

The Portuguese romanized the city's name as Malacca. For a while, it continued to serve as a center of trade, part of a network of Portuguese-controlled Asian ports: Goa, Cochin, Colombo, Ternate, Macau, and so on (Subrahmanyam 1993). A fortress, churches, and monasteries were added to the cityscape, but trade fell off sharply as Portuguese discrimination against Muslim merchants and imposition of state monopolies lessened the city's attractions as an entrepôt. By the mid-seventeenth century, the Dutch had helped the sultan of the nearby state of Johor, a descendent of the Melaka ruling house, to drive the Portuguese out of the city. Although the Sultan of Johor gave the Dutch control over Melaka, Dutch warships policed the Straits from their Asian headquarters in Batavia, on the northwestern coast of Java, and Melaka lost population and wealth.

In exchange for a defensive alliance against Siam, in 1786, the Malayan Sultan of Kedah had granted Britain the island of Penang, on the western approach to the Straits, on which they founded George Town (Figure 1). During the Napoleonic era (1798–1815), the British and French fought each other across the globe, everywhere with the assistance of local allies (Jasanoff 2005). Napoleon's defeat of the Netherlands in Europe led Britain to occupy Batavia, giving it control over the Straits in the early nineteenth century. The French defeat in 1815 allowed Britain to expand its presence in Asia; in the early 1820s, Britain gained sovereignty over Singapore via a treaty with the leaders of Johor. The British opened the port of Singapore to merchants of all countries, and it gradually supplanted Malacca as the regional trade center over several subsequent decades. The state of Johor provided Singapore what Malacca had lacked: a base for agricultural products, harvested by Chinese workers recruited by the state's Malay leaders (Barr 2019).

Anthony Reid notes that, in the early decades of European conquest, the new masters of Asia's port cities adopted many of the economic and social practices long present in places like Melaka, including rituals establishing social hierarchy and sumptuary rules to make hierarchy visible. Labor was secured by purchasing workers. Although Europeans referred to such people as "slaves," the difficulty of preventing them from running away or attacking their masters meant that European employers generally had to treat their "property" in ways that conformed to local custom. Gradually, however, as their power grew, European colonial authorities gained the "ability to impose a uniform legal system on their inhabitants" and began to dominate the social order (Reid 1999: 195–96). The growing use of stone and brick in constructing forts, churches,

Figure 1 Two early twentieth-century stereoscopic views of Penang. Top: *Penang, from Anchorage in the Harbor – Off the Malayan Peninsula, West* (1901). New York: Underwood & Underwood. Source: www.loc.gov/item/2020639372/. Bottom: *Loading Freight into Native Buffalo Carts at the Waterfront, Penang, Straits Settlement* (1907). Chicago: H.C. White. Source: www .loc.gov/item/2020639366/

official buildings, and residences indicated the wealth of the European city-builders and signaled their intent to maintain their dominance (Andaya 1999: 19). The British government of Singapore paid for its infrastructure and staff salaries by selling to "tax farmers" the right to tax opium and other commodities and services (Trocki 1990).

The names and histories of the European adventurers who conquered Asian territory have long been famous in Anglophone history. They include, among others: Jan Pieterszoon Coen, founder of Batavia on the island of Java; Robert Clive, who established Calcutta as the Asian headquarters of the British East

India Company; and Stamford Raffles of Singapore. All of them succeeded by taking advantage of rivalries between powerful local rulers, allying with one or the other, providing military and other assistance, and thereby establishing a foothold to build from. Their local allies adopted aspects of the culture of the outsiders, a phenomenon that had recurred throughout history, from early periods of Indian influence within Southeast Asian courts to the spread of Islam (de Casparis and Mabbett 1999). To some extent, the activities of Christian missionaries and European merchants in Asia fit old patterns.

The quality of European influence in early modern Southeast Asia, however, differed from that of earlier waves of cultural change because it was supported by strong states seeking military and economic dominance in an atmosphere of intense interstate competition. The Dutch and British governments chartered East Indies companies and gave them trade monopolies and the power to wage war to consolidate control over Asian territory. Still, although the Europeans were clearly military conquerors, they offered opportunities to ambitious Asians to take up positions within their regimes, and the urban and economic development they promoted appealed to many Asian entrepreneurs. In the case of the Straits colonial cities, Chinese and Indian businessmen and workers quickly outnumbered Malay and European residents, although Europeans set the rules and enforced them. The distinctive militaristic and developmentalist nature of European expansion into the Indian Ocean world is visible in the history of European-controlled Asian cities.

2.2 European Port Cities in Asia and Their Influence

Even before the modern city concept was introduced into European colonies in Asia in the late nineteenth century, certain features of urbanizing Europe's culture and social thought gained advocates among Asian intellectuals. Their promotion of these new ideals and practices helped legitimize colonial rule even as it called into being conservative opposition and newly articulated ideas of cultural identity. Rammohan Roy (1772–1833) is a striking example of such a figure in Indian history.

A native of Bengal, Rammohan Roy rebelled against parental expectations and sought out a broad education, including in the principles of European philosophy, Christianity, Buddhism, and Islam. His studies led him to conclude that his Brahmin family and other practitioners of what the British called "Hinduism" had distorted the wisdom of the ancient classics they claimed to revere. He praised British society for valuing intellectual inquiry and promoting literacy. After working as a translator for the British East India Company, Roy founded Bengali- and Persian-language newspapers in Calcutta in 1821 and fought against colonial restrictions on the press. Most controversially, he criticized the subjugation of women in Indian communities, especially the practice of *sati*. The expectation that widows would throw themselves on their husbands' funeral pyres, he argued, was a perversion of classical teachings about conjugal relations. His campaign urging the British to outlaw *sati* made him notorious among some circles in India but helped jumpstart a social reform movement that spread from his base in Calcutta to other Indian cities. He established a society dedicated to the study of religion and open to all, providing a model for many similar associational initiatives in later years (Guha 2011: 23–44).

Rammohan Roy is clearly an exceptional figure in many ways, but his interest in the opportunities that came with changing times was not uncommon. The colonial cities Europeans commanded attracted many migrants. Table 1 provides rough population estimates for some of these cities, as well as other cities in Asia. European economic ambitions for their colonies in Asia led them to recruit workers and managers from near and far to build houses and transportation infrastructure, plant and harvest crops, work in factories, and load ships. In the cities, these migrants often settled in ethnic enclaves. Following old practices of Southeast Asian rulers, the European regimes recognized headmen of each ethnic community who were expected to maintain the peace and manage disputes, keeping expenses low for the colonial government. Thus, a "Kapitan China" was recognized as the mediator between colonial authorities and the large Chinese communities that grew up in cities such as Spanish Manila, Dutch Batavia, and British Penang.

The segregation of populations in colonial cities by ethnicity, class, caste, gender, and religion was pervasive but varied over time. Carl Nightingale argues that, in the case of the British empire, late eighteenth-century pseudo-scientific concepts of racial hierarchy offered new justifications for existing practices and led to new measures to separate whites from Asians in Indian cities such as Calcutta. In that center of commerce and industry, though, money broke down some of the boundaries between the British and Bengalis. Although clubs and some public venues were restricted by "race," many of the palatial homes originally built for white managers of the East India Company ended up in the hands of wealthy Bengalis. Segregation was most marked and vigorously policed in the towns the British built as military bases (cantonments) and in the "hill stations" such as Simla, where wealthy Britons escaped the summer heat. Still, indigenous servants and other staff accompanied white families on their travels (Nightingale 2012). Mixed marriages produced "Eurasians," "métis," and other multicultural families, challenging ideas about fixed racial identities and hierarchies (Ghosh 2006; Taylor 2009; Pillai 2015).

Table 1 Approximate population figures for select Asian cities

| City | Approximate population at about the year | | | | | | | UN estimate |
	1850	1900	1925	1950	1975	2000	2018	2030
Bombay/Mumbai	580,000	780,000	1,170,000	2,680,000	7,000,000	16,147,000	19,980,000	24,572,000
Calcutta/Kolkata	413,182	1,085,000	1,390,000	4,800,000	7,800,000	13,097,000	14,681,000	17,584,000
Delhi (Old and New)	156,000	207,000	375,000	1,306,000	4,400,000	15,692,000	28,514,000	38,939,000
Singapore	60,000	193,000	485,000	740,000	2,200,000	3,914,000	5,792,000	6,342,000
Bangkok	158,000	200,000	375,000	975,000	4,300,000	6,395,000	10,156,000	12,101,000
Batavia/Jakarta	60,000	115,000	290,000	1,452,000	5,300,000	8,390,000	10,517,000	12,687,000
Saigon/Ho Chi Minh City	50,000	170,000	329,000	1,200,000	3,500,000	4,389,000	8,145,000	11,054,000
Manila	114,000	190,000	325,000	1,400,000	5,400,000	9,958,000	13,482,000	16,841,000
Hong Kong	33,000	192,000	750,000	2,100,000	3,900,000	6,664,000	7,429,000	7,987,000
Shanghai	185,000	619,000	1,500,000	5,406,000	8,000,000	14,247,000	25,582,000	32,869,000
Beijing	1,648,000	1,100,000	1,266,000	2,031,000	5,200,000	10,285,000	19,618,000	24,282,000
Seoul	183,000	195,000	297,000	1,550,000	6,800,000	9,879,000	9,963,000	10,163,000
Tokyo	780,000	1,497,000	5,300,000	7,000,000	23,000,000	34,450,000	37,468,000	36,574,000

Note: Figures are approximate, and definition of urban population varies by city and time; see the explanation in Reba, Reitsama, and Seto (2016).
Sources: Figures for 2000, 2018, and 2030 are from The World's Cities in 2018, a component of United Nations, Department of Economic and Social Affairs, Population Division (2018).
Except for Hong Kong and Singapore, the figures for 1850 as well as 1900–1975 are from Reba, Reitsama, and Seto (2018). The figure for Hong Kong in 1850 is from Morris (2011). The figure for Singapore in 1850 is from Trocki (2006).

By the late nineteenth century, European-dominated cities were flourishing across much of Asia. The British had moved into the interior of Burma and India, taking over populous Mughal administrative capitals such as Delhi and Lucknow (Heitzman 2008; Beverley 2011). The Spanish had imposed city forms developed in Latin America in the Philippines (Morley 2018a), and Dutch colonial cities in Indonesia replicated many urban features of the home country (Blussé 2013). The modern city concept burst onto the scene in the 1890s and transformed both ideas about cities and cities themselves across Asia, beginning in the urban bases of colonial administration.

2.3 The Expansion of Municipal Authority and the Creation of the Modern City in Colonial Asia

The concept of the modern city emerged in large part from the work of a new type of professional: urban planners. Carola Hein (2018: 2) notes that the work of planning was "conceived as a rational, modernist pursuit for societal improvement in response to the urban ills produced by the industrial revolution." The city – its structures, population, economy, and so on – began to be reenvisioned as an integrated whole in the process of planning. Colonial cities were important testing grounds for European urban planners because the highly militarized colonial state often commanded more authority in such cities than metropolitan governments did in cities at home. Some urban reform techniques pioneered in Calcutta, such as slum clearance to make way for upscale development that would finance new public infrastructure, were introduced subsequently in London (Nightingale 2012; Datta 2013; Harris 2020).

Another key factor in the coalescence of the idea of the modern city was the rapidity of technological change implemented in cities in the decades before and after 1900, the era of the so-called Second Industrial Revolution (Adas 2014: 141–42). Trains reshaped cities as the areas around stations attracted commerce. Streetcar lines expanded urban boundaries at the same time that electrification opened up huge disparities between urban and rural life. Electricity facilitated industry, including new cultural industries such as film, while making public nightlife possible. Film and various types of print media, in turn, promoted images of the city as both attractive and dangerous. Modern industry and culture also required a different sense of time – clock time – and sped up the pace of daily life (Adas 2014: 61–62, 224). Electricity energized the modern city materially and metaphorically. New urban technologies invented in Europe or the United States quickly made their way to factories and ports in Asian cities (Hausman, Hertner, and Wilkins 2008: 123).

Innovative urban technologies spread to colonial cities for the same reasons they were adopted in metropolitan cities. They promised to increase productivity and profit while providing ways to address the challenges that came to be associated with rapidly growing industrial cities: disease and crime. The need to promote proper hygiene was interpreted in colonial cities as a moral as well as a physical matter. Ann Stoler (2020) and Philippa Levine (2004) argue that regulating sexual contact between colonizers and colonized was a core concern of European imperial administrators, who feared the possible "corruption" of their "civilization" due to the exposure of their citizens to colonial "deviance." Clean, well-managed cities – where production and transportation were not disrupted by disease, crime, or moral turpitude – were considered by imperial and local authorities to be critical for international prestige (Harris 2020). Municipal governments expanded to manage the new infrastructure, changing the relationship between the colonial powers and their subjects. Cooptation of local leaders into urban governance to improve its efficacy eventually contributed to the rise of nationalist movements in many colonial cities across Asia.

2.3.1 Funding Urban Infrastructure

From the beginning, colonial regimes were determined to find local resources to fund their growing settlements in Asia. Some public infrastructure in colonial cities – roads and walls and government offices – was constructed using convict labor (Yang 2003). In nineteenth-century Singapore, British authorities sold the right to collect taxes on opium and other products and services to tax farmers, generally heads of Chinese organizations: *kongsi*, translated by some historians as syndicates. The income gained by delegating authority to tax farmers may have been sufficient to fund port improvements and other basic infrastructure, but the rapid growth of colonial cities in the late nineteenth century began to present serious management challenges. As in crowded industrial cities in Europe and America, health concerns motivated the expansion of municipal government to enable it to adopt more intrusive regulation, such as housing and sanitation codes, and put in place expensive public health measures, such as water supply systems and sewers. Wherever this expansion of government authority occurred, it was never a smooth process. Racism fed into power asymmetries to create especially challenging conditions in colonial cities, however.

Brenda Yeoh's detailed study of the expansion of municipal authority in Singapore reveals a colonial discourse of urban improvement based on racist cultural assumptions and designed to justify imposing the costs of regulation and reform on Asian residents. On the question of waste disposal, for example,

British officials claimed that collecting human waste in latrines for transport by pails to collection points was superior to installing a more expensive pipe system because, in their view, Asians cared little for cleanliness and would surely damage complicated equipment. Yeoh writes, "Confusing cause with effect, the sanitary habits of Asians were perceived not as an adaptation to the want of proper facilities, but a failure of their civilization, a view which only served to confirm racial prejudices and to heighten the sense that the Asians were indeed a race apart, as much removed from the rudiments of modern civilization as they were from the respectability of water-closets" (Yeoh 1996: 205).

Curiously enough, Yeoh notes, at the time the decision in favor of pails was made, Singapore's municipal government had already solicited a report on waste disposal in other parts of the British empire and had learned that the major cities in India and Burma, as well as nearby Chinese-majority Penang and Hong Kong, had already established sewer systems. So, while it is clear that much information was shared among colonial municipal authorities, local conditions – particular personalities and prejudices, in addition to social and geographic factors – resulted in variations in urban development across cities. In Singapore, Yeoh points out, British authorities feared the power of the Chinese syndicates that organized labor, including waste haulers. Strikes and protests over increased taxes and regulation could shut down the city. The British had little understanding of or influence over these powerful Chinese associations and a strong desire to avoid provoking them. Colonial authorities in Penang and Hong Kong faced somewhat similar environments, but there they seem to have been able to work more effectively with local elites to find ways to fund expensive infrastructure such as water and sewer systems (Carroll 2005; Lees 2017).

In French Indochina, early urban planning was carried out by the military, and the architectural forms adopted were strictly French (Wright 1991). The colonial government brought in prefabricated iron bridges and building components, supplied by the Eiffel company and other Paris manufacturers, as well as dredging machines to cut canals through the Mekong Delta, connecting Saigon more firmly to its hinterland. The costs were recouped from the profits of sugar and rice plantations that the new infrastructure made possible (Biggs 2010).

The Spaniards who ruled the Philippines showed less interest in modern city infrastructure. At the time of their defeat by Filipino anti-colonial forces in 1898, the only sizable city, Manila, had an inadequate water supply and a very minimal sewer system that emptied into the moat around the walled center of town, built for Spaniards. American officials justified their subsequent takeover of the Philippines in part because of how "backward" Manila and its port were in terms of technology (Morley 2018a). Municipal development was also not a high priority in the Netherlands East Indies. Municipal councils were set up early in the twentieth century, but goals were modest, and public infrastructure primarily benefited the European residents (Silver 2008; Coté 2014). Abidin Kusno (2000) argues, however, that Dutch attempts in the late colonial period to represent local cultures in the forms of new buildings and urban planning – an effort to show interest in local traditions and thereby shore up the legitimacy of their rule – left a significant legacy, establishing parameters for national identity construction in the postcolonial period.

2.3.2 Policing Colonial Cities

Concerns about health and disease in growing cities pushed the expansion of policing, in addition to the construction of sanitation infrastructure, since intrusive regulations on housing, business, and street life required mechanisms for surveillance and enforcement. While the leadership of colonial policing agencies remained in the hands of Europeans, the vast majority of the constables themselves were colonized subjects. Colonial authorities adopted various strategies for maximizing the usefulness of police forces while minimizing the threat they posed to colonial rule.

Before the late nineteenth century, ethnic and religious communities were allowed and encouraged to handle their own affairs in many colonial cities. In much of Southeast Asia and in Hong Kong, Chinese syndicates and native-place or brotherhood associations organized markets and settled disputes, sometimes violently. Colonial regimes looked the other way unless European interests were threatened. The ever-present military could be called in to deal with serious unrest, although that could also pose a threat, as the British found out when Indian troops rose up against them in 1857.

Prashant Kidambi (2007) points out that Indian constables in Bombay were recruited from working-class neighborhoods and tended to use their local connections to address problems informally. In the 1890s, though, the municipal government's forceful efforts to deal with a plague epidemic heightened the tensions between the police and Bombay's neighborhoods, calling into question the extent to which ordinary constables would enforce city policies. Municipal authorities then attempted to build up the professional identity of the police force in order to strengthen its loyalty to the government and lessen its susceptibility to community influences. The Bombay Improvement Trust, established in 1910, was officially intended as a mechanism to demolish slums while simultaneously increasing the supply of affordable housing. It provided very little new housing for those forced from the demolished slum areas but did manage to accommodate the police, building houses for "26 European officers, 38 Indian officers, and 538 constables and their families" (Kidambi 2007: 78).

In the Netherlands East Indies, the government also adopted policies aimed at professionalizing the police in the early twentieth century, to address fears and complaints about collusion with antiestablishment forces (criminal gangs, in the government's terms). The rise of armed resistance to Dutch rule in the late 1910s, though, shifted attention from municipal regulation and neighborhood policing to the creation of a General Investigation Service to function across the colonial territory. This centralized police bureau had the power to censor publications, restrict assembly, and investigate suspicious persons and groups. Police agents were recruited from outside the districts in which they were to serve but within the same linguistic region, and officers were Europeans, for the most part (Shiraishi 2003). Similarly, in Indochina, the police force "seemed to have its tentacles everywhere" (McHale 2004: 42). As in Indonesia and the British empire, people recruited into the colonial civil service in one region were often sent to manage affairs in other parts of the colony. Vietnamese officers sent to Cambodia and Laos themselves often adopted a superior attitude toward the locals (Goscha 2016: 118–21).

2.3.3 Municipal Expansion and Changing Relations between Colonizer and Colonized

The growing ambition of municipal authorities to transform urban life through physical and social engineering – including slum clearance, health inspections, higher taxes, and more intrusive policing – raised the visibility of city government and changed its relationship with the people it governed. The British established Improvement Trusts in large cities across their empire with the aim, as noted by Partho Datta (2013: 139), "to limit the influence of local residents" so as to "enact the schemes of British-trained experts, notably those of a nascent planning profession, in ways that were insulated from potential opposition." Formal municipal corporations, which had long included indigenous representatives, lost power over city affairs to these new professional bodies. Local newspapers and associations, however, amplified residents' views on municipal policy, and new regulations were sometimes challenged in colonial courts as well as the court of public opinion.

As Lynn Lees (2017: 125) argues in respect to cities in British Malaya: "The administrative weaknesses of municipal colonial governments opened the door for complaints by residents, who sometimes turned the demand for better public health and sanitation against the British. Sanitary and health reforms, rather than disciplining British subjects, brought their voices into a local political process, albeit a non-representative one." This was true also in French Indochina and the Netherlands East Indies (McHale 2004; Dick and Rimmer 2013; Metcalf 2013). In Kidambi's view (2013: 567), "for all their limitations, it was in the domain of municipal politics that Indian educated elites first began to contest the iniquities and exclusions of colonial rule." By the late nineteenth century, in India, this contestation was conducted largely in English and led by lawyers and other professionals who had been educated to accept British ideals (Haynes 1991).

Expanding municipal services drew colonial authorities into local disputes. Kidambi (2007) shows this in his analysis of neighborhood associations in Bombay that called on the colonial police to suppress religious parades, leading to violent protests that required more policing. Khoo Salma Nasution (2002) uncovers a similar dynamic in Penang, where local notables endowed a type of charitable fund (*waqf*) common in Muslim communities. When disputes arose about the use of *waqf* property, the British colonial government established a Board for Muslim and Hindu Charities, appointing members it saw as sympathetic to its own development goals. The board operated much as improvement trusts did in other cities, managing the *waqf* property and devoting the income to a wide range of civic and religious purposes that the *waqf* founders could not have foreseen.

By the time the United States took over the Philippines in 1898, the European imperial powers had long incorporated a select group of the colonized into formal governance structures. According to Paul Kramer (2006: 151), the American conquerors immediately realized that "in very practical terms, the best way to guarantee stability was to surrender large portions of the state to powerful Filipinos who had formerly resisted the U.S. invasion." Municipal government quickly became the purview of large landholders, although American officials retained significant fiscal control. American engineering firms and advertisers laid claim to Manila's streetscape, as may be seen in Figure 2.

Within a few years of its establishment, the US administration in the Philippines hired Chicago-based Daniel Burnham to create a master plan for Manila and a new city in the mountains – Baguio, an American version of the hill station. Ian Morley (2018a) argues that, by creating vistas and green spaces that were open to all, Burnham's plan strove to break down ethnic divisions maintained under Spanish rule and encourage all residents to identify with the city. US authorities also erected a monument to José Rizal, executed by the Spanish in 1896, in a plaza in the center of Manila, celebrating him as a patriot. Such urban design gestures may have been meant to signal US intentions merely to "assist" the Filipinos to build their own unified nation, but, as Kramer (2006: 362–63) notes, racism permeated American rule as the colonizers and their local allies tried to justify an extended colonial occupation. Still, Morley (2018b)

STREET SPRINKLING—THE NEW WAY.

Figure 2 The new US-dominated Municipal Board of Manila celebrated innovations in street management. In this photo, electrical lines have been strung, and an advertisement for American beer looms in the background. Source: Municipal Board (1905). *Annual Report for 1904* (Manila: Municipal Board), photograph between pages 240 and 241

argues, by the 1920s, Filipino planners and architects, some trained in the United States, had begun to take a lead in urban design in the provinces, continuing Burnham's City Beautiful movement in their own ways.

Municipal coalitions that brought together colonial officials and local elites in pursuit of urban development faced ongoing challenges and required frequent renegotiation, as will be examined in the context of the rise of anti-colonial movements in Section 4. Local taxpayers and city residents were not the only ones to criticize municipal government. Kramer (2006: 153) notes that American businessmen who flocked to Manila in the early twentieth century complained about the employment of Filipinos in many government positions. Within the British empire, as with the Vietnamese in Indochina, Asian urban professionals and police were sent around the empire to manage the affairs and regulate the lives of people whose languages and cultures were unfamiliar to them (Metcalf 2007). Sometimes, though, they became community leaders in their new homes, as was the case with Hafiz Ghulam Sarwar (1873–1954), best known to history as the first Sunni Muslim to translate the Qur'an into English. Sarwar was a Punjabi trained in math and philology at Cambridge University and appointed to the Malayan Civil Service, serving as sheriff of Penang and as a judge in Singapore. After a career that lasted almost thirty years, he retired to devote himself to scholarship, public speaking, and community service, including as a Rotarian, in George Town, Penang. And many others followed similar trajectories (Nasution 2002; Wazir 2009; Lees 2017: 301–3).

2.3.4 Imperial Showplaces

To enhance the prestige of the colonizers, colonial cities needed the accoutrements of the modern city and imperial grandeur. This topic has been very well covered in the literature. The 1911 transfer of the capital of British India from Calcutta to Delhi, former seat of the Mughal dynasty, is a prime example. The British constructed the government buildings of New Delhi in a new "Indo-Saracenic" style over the next two decades to imply cultural continuity between Mughal and British authority (Chopra 2016). British consultants also developed new central plans for other administrative centers in India, although the most famous of these planners – Patrick Geddes – deemphasized imperial pomp in favor of sensitivity to local concerns in his work in India between 1915 and 1922 (Rao-Cavale 2017). Burnham's plan for Manila (Section 2.3.3), like Geddes's work, consciously rejected the pomp of New Delhi and other colonial capitals, paying homage to Filipino patriotism while incorporating elements of the layouts of Chicago and Cleveland.

In Indochina, Hanoi was designated the new capital in 1897, in part, as in the case of Delhi, because it was a former capital of a displaced dynasty and thus "embodied an aristocratic air of tranquil refinement," in contrast to merchant-dominated Saigon (Vann 2007: 283). But French colonial rule suffered from the instability of the home government. "In Indochina even more than in metropolitan France, the instability and weakness of political authority encouraged grandiose and vain acts of assertiveness. Civic architecture tried to convey the impression of authority and continuity where they by no means existed" (Wright 1991: 166).

Public events celebrating empire, including festivities to welcome visiting notables, attracted large crowds in colonial cities. In Malayan cities, parades, sporting events, and essay contests encouraged residents to commemorate royal birthdays and coronations. Enthusiastic participation did not necessarily signal strong loyalty to the throne, however (Lees 2017: 284–87).

Postcolonial Asian regimes had to deal with the lingering impact of symbolism in the colonial city, as we will see in Section 5. The colonial stamp could most clearly be seen in these cities. Effacing it by transforming cities into new symbols of the nation became a priority across Asia.

2.4 Social Life in Colonial Cities: Cosmopolitanism and Urban Identities

Heterogeneity characterized modern colonial cities. Over the course of time, migrants formed insular communities but also came together in public spaces. The nature of these experiences varied by class, caste, ethnicity, gender, sexuality, and religious affiliation, as well as intersectionally. City life shaped consciousness in complicated ways. All people who lived in a city with running water and electricity, however, were aware that they were living in a modern city, even if they could not afford to make use of them. The discursive environment of modern city life – regulations posted by police, public celebrations of empire, proselytizing by religious associations, public protests, and so on – was unavoidable. The question of how various people responded to the idea of the modern city will be taken up more directly in Section 4. Here, I will briefly share a sampling of insights from the extensive scholarship on the formation of urban identities in colonial cities.

Scholars who write about Chinese residents of colonial cities – in Hong Kong as well as Southeast and South Asia – have pointed to cemeteries as an interesting indicator of urban identity. In the past, many Chinese strongly believed, and some continue to believe, that after death one's body should be buried near the ancestral home, in part so that family members can maintain the grave, a key way to ensure happiness in the afterlife and good fortune to survivors. Elizabeth Sinn (2013) shows that nineteenth-century Hong Kong became a transit point for tens of thousands of remains repatriated from abroad, including San Francisco. But, as Chinese communities grew in colonial cities, and particularly as families formed and branched out, native-place associations and other groups bought cemetery land in their cities of residence. Ties to hometowns in China often persisted, but Penang and Singapore and Hong Kong and Calcutta also came to be considered home (Yeoh 1996: chapter 8; Nasution 2002; Carroll 2005: 113–14; Zhang and Sen 2012). That was particularly the case for the Peranakan Chinese, a community formed as a result of marriages between Chinese men and Malay women (Keo 2020).

Print culture and schools contributed much to the formation of urban identities in colonial cities. In reference to Indochina, Shawn McHale (2004: 151) shows that publishing gradually moved from "small centers of knowledge" such as Buddhist temples to concentrate in the major cities, where secular publishing flourished. Philippe Peycam (2013: 507) notes that "disparities in access to Western education inevitably led to social separation between people who were unschooled, those educated at traditional village schools, those educated at Franco-Vietnamese schools, and those educated at French schools." Saigon journalists, many of whom had received a French education, argued that city dwellers had a moral obligation to "defend their rural compatriots," the "backward" common people, from colonial oppression – a sign that they had developed a consciousness of urban superiority (Peycam 2013: 519).

As centers of industry and trade, colonial cities tended to attract more men than women, and their populations fluctuated seasonally and in other ways, as demand for labor rose and fell. The most prominent and influential sector of the new, technologically advanced cities of the early twentieth century was the growing middle class comprising professionals such as teachers, lawyers, accountants, technicians, physicians, and journalists. For the middle-class residents of Asian colonial cities, choices abounded and identities were malleable, as Su Lin Lewis argues in her study of Bangkok, Penang, and Rangoon. Among these communities, she notes, English served as an "inter-Asian language" that allowed for civic life across ethnic borders (2016: 32). At the same time, urban life heightened the consciousness of difference, which some city residents cultivated. Writing about Bombay in the decades around 1900, Kidambi (2007: 167) observes that "a noteworthy feature of associational life in the city in those years was the growth of societies and clubs that were based on putatively 'ascribed' identities of caste and religious community, but were in fact an outcome of conscious choices made by individuals within a modernizing urban environment." Such ascriptive association by choice was often strengthened during the difficult history of anti-colonial struggle and has shaped postcolonial urban life as well.

2.5 Modern Cities of Colonial Asia as of 1930

Despite variations across and within empires, by around 1900 modern cities – cities with sophisticated infrastructure, intensive policing, professional staff, and governance systems that to some degree involved local stakeholders – had emerged throughout colonial Asia. After an initial push to respond to disease outbreaks and other challenges between 1890 and 1914, developments generally slowed during WWI, as the European powers redirected resources to the battlefields. The pace picked up once again in the 1920s. By then, Japan had become a leading imperial power and played a significant role in international conferences in an era that can be considered the height of global preoccupation with municipal reform, as Section 3 will argue.

The modern city as a concept became more pervasive in parallel with the emergence of modern colonial cities, as did the feeling among city populations that they belonged to it, as participants in its neighborhoods and associational life. This latter phenomenon has been studied most fully in the case of the new middle classes, but evidence points to a broad cultural impact on people's understanding of space and public life. In the 1930s, anti-colonial movements fixed attention on the nation rather than the city. Significant developments in urban administration and governance continued, but they were not as visible to the increasingly restive colonial publics as they had been in earlier decades. Most notably, strong critiques of the modern city both as an idea and as a material manifestation fueled anti-colonial activism, which we will examine in Section 4.

3 Emulation and Innovation in Cities Controlled by Asians before WWII

Comparing the evolution of cities in China, Japan, and Europe between 1600 and 1800, historian William Rowe (2013: 325) emphasizes striking similarities: rising consciousness of differences in rural and urban life, flourishing print cultures and venues for socializing and performance, geographic mobility, and the growth of associations that managed many aspects of social life. In short, he argues that "early modern urbanism was indeed a Eurasian, if not global, phenomenon." Although I argue in this Element that a new "modern city" concept was introduced in Asia as a decidedly foreign import, Rowe's point must be borne in mind. Huge, complex cities are by no means a recent development in Asia. That many Asian regimes were familiar with the challenges faced by urbanization and densely populated urban centers served to heighten their interest in the modern city vision when it coalesced in the 1890s. Rulers of Asian polities that managed to resist European colonization found the technological advances and many of the governance practices associated with the Euro-American conception of the modern city – such as professionalized police – very attractive. Many of them promoted the modern city vision in their own territories, domesticating it for their own cultural environments.

The distinction made in this section and Section 2 between colonial cities and cities controlled by Asians is useful, I believe, but too simplistic. As noted in Section 2, colonial cities were not completely dominated by the colonizers. The growing professional class of Asian residents of colonial cities increasingly took on managerial roles and ownership over these cities as the twentieth century progressed. Asian regimes that avoided colonization, on the other hand, were not entirely free to operate as they wished. Colonial powers demanded access to markets and changes in legal systems to protect foreign life and property, backing up their demands with military threats and even invasion. Vladimir Lenin coined the term "semi-colony" to describe this phenomenon, but that term – although it is frequently used in the context of Chinese history (Yang 2019) – only gestures toward the wide range of relationships that Asian polities built with the imperial powers in the late nineteenth and early twentieth centuries. This section illustrates the complexity of changes in cities in a number of uncolonized Asian realms in that era and reveals the widespread impact of the modern city concept in these spaces.

3.1 Cities among and between Empires

Hyderabad, long one of India's most populous cities, was not incorporated into the British empire but was recognized by the British as one of the hundreds of "princely states" entirely surrounded by their empire. Such more or less autonomous "minor states," as Eric Beverley calls them, also existed in British Malaya and the Netherlands East Indies. British and Dutch officials (residents) were posted to many of them as advisers. In his study of Hyderabad, Beverley (2015: 19) notes that "Hyderabad and other minor states took up the emerging 'major' political language of the modern state (dominated by European nation-states and empires) as a way to assert their authority." But Beverley shows that, while Hyderabad's rulers were committed to expanding the state – including in ways associated with the modern city – they chose to look beyond the British empire for ideas about how to develop their territory, hiring experts from around the world and attempting to infuse Islamic ethical ideals into urban planning schemes. The provision of public housing for the poor was emphasized and even realized to an unusual extent.

The rulers of Siam (renamed Thailand in 1939) maintained their country's sovereignty by adroit negotiation with the rivalrous French and British, as well as via effective centralizing efforts. Mongkut, who ruled in the 1850s and 1860s as King Rama IV, brought European surveyors into the realm, both to help design the capital at Bangkok and to claim territory for Siam within carefully mapped borders, thus creating the nation's "geo-body," as explained by Thongchai Winichakul (1994). As Bangkok developed in the late nineteenth and early twentieth centuries, it came to resemble colonial cities such as Rangoon, with ethnically diverse and growing professional and merchant communities (Lewis 2016). C. A. Trocki (1999: 120–21), though, points out that the close connection between the Thai royal family and Buddhist institutions made Bangkok a religious center in a way that no colonial city could be and provided avenues of communication between ruler and subject that did not depend on modern technologies or modern schools. Nevertheless, the Thai rulers promoted modern technology and schools, in addition to Buddhism. Elites in Siam believed in the necessity to "keep up with the times" in areas such as urban infrastructure, believing that modern cities were the measure of "civilization" (*siwilai*), as well as centers of spiritual authority (Thongchai 2000).

Colonial powers established urban enclaves even in territory claimed by the most powerful and cohesive Asian states, Tokugawa Japan and Qing China. Before the mid-nineteenth century, small settlements at Nagasaki and Guangzhou allowed European merchants to engage in tightly regulated trade. The 1842 Treaty of Nanjing that ended the First Opium War between the Qing and Britain, along with subsequent treaties, granted control of sections of dozens of coastal and riverine cities in China to the British and other foreigners – the so-called foreign concessions in "treaty ports." Three of these treaty ports – Guangzhou, Shanghai, and Tianjin – quickly attracted large populations, including wealthy Chinese interested in the amenities of modern cities (Rowe 2013). American pressure in Japan led in the 1850s to the establishment of a similar settlement in Yokohama, near the shogun's capital, Edo (Chaiklin 2012). In response, a top-down revolution led by discontented samurai in the name of the emperor overthrew the shogun in 1868, at which point Emperor Meiji and his imperial house were relocated from Kyoto to Edo, renamed Tokyo. A rapid program of military modernization, industrialization, and urbanization allowed Japan's new government to regain sovereignty over foreign settlements by the 1890s and tariff autonomy in 1911. At that point, the Japanese had already launched their own colonization efforts in neighboring territories, including Korea and Taiwan.

3.2 Defensive Nationalism and Conceptions of the City in the Japanese Empire

In the Meiji period (1868–1910), the Japanese state undertook a life-or-death struggle to avoid the sort of foreign dominance it saw being imposed on nearby China. The Meiji leaders chose a strategy of learning from their rivals, the Western powers, just as an earlier generation of Japanese rulers had studied Chinese statecraft – including urban planning – in order to consolidate and strengthen the state. Debates over what aspects of foreign culture needed to be promoted proliferated; all aspects of American and European life were scrutinized, including urban planning, infrastructure, and governance. The government hired foreign experts to advise it on railroad construction and many other new initiatives; Japanese students received support to study these subjects in Europe and the United States (Sorensen 2002: 50). At the same time, though, it articulated and implemented a vision of a distinctive Japanese urban tradition. The imperial family moved from Kyoto to the extensive grounds of the former shogunal residence, which, while well screened from the public, sat at the heart of Tokyo. Kyoto, with its many old temples, shrines, and entertainment venues, was reconstructed and revered as the wellspring of Japanese imperial culture (Tseng 2018).

In Tokyo, Meiji authorities benefited from the availability of large parcels of land – the property of former regional lords (daimyo) who had been obliged to spend half their time in Edo in attendance on the shogun (Waley 2013). In addition to these estates, the government claimed a swath of central-city land that had been devastated by fire to build a new commercial center of European-style brick buildings: the famous Ginza, designed in the 1870s by a British architect. This model development served as a visual advertisement of Japan's aim to be modern. Few local builders working in the city made the shift from wooden to brick construction, however, despite the government's encourage-ment. As André Sorensen (2002: 40) observes, the Japanese vernacular building tradition valued wood for building and "continued to provide the image of ideal urban housing long after modernisation had introduced dramatic changes in other aspects of Japanese culture such as clothing." Tokyo's population boomed in the early twentieth century, but most residents lived in densely packed neighborhoods that continued to suffer from fire, particularly in the wake of a 1923 earthquake (Seidensticker 1991; Huffman 2018).

In regard to governance, the Japanese sent official delegations abroad to observe administration in Europe and the United States and translated moun-tains of textbooks and regulations. Remarkably quickly, new urban-centered institutions such as police, a postal service, and public schools were designed and staffed. In 1889, Emperor Meiji promulgated a new constitution; regula-tions to guide the growth of cities appeared about the same time. Japanese officials prided themselves not on adopting foreign policies wholesale but on analyzing the strengths and weaknesses of the "civilized" world and combining aspects of its best features, not neglecting to include older Japanese practices judged useful (Westney 1987). Modernization that had begun in defensive mode soon morphed into a source of national pride, with new textbooks celebrating Japanese unity in the quest to become powerful and wealthy.

By the 1890s, along with their counterparts in Europe and America, many Japanese intellectuals and officials understood cities as key drivers of eco-nomic growth and prioritized investment in infrastructure to benefit industry (Sorensen 2002). Jeffrey Hanes's 2002 study of Seki Hajime, an economist who in the 1920s became mayor of Osaka – Japan's second-largest city and a center of industry and trade – shows that some Japanese thinkers stayed in close touch with the social reformers of the United States and Western Europe. Seki's conception of cities, Hanes shows, shifted along with his reading of progressive social theory. From seeing cities as economic engines, objects that could be tinkered with to improve productivity, he began to see them as communities made up of the diverse members of the national family. Some family members, he noted, had not benefited from the economic growth that peaked during WWI, and in consequence their protests ravaged the city during the subsequent recession. As mayor, inspired by, but also critical of, Britain's utopian Garden City concept, he tried to manage the growth of Osaka by developing public transit and comfortable neighborhoods for workers. The central government and business interests thwarted most of his plans, however. Many Japanese elites claimed that labor unrest, which Seki feared, would not become a problem as it had in Europe and the United States. Even when confronted by journalists' exposés of substandard housing and other urban miseries, many Japanese officials were confident that Japanese culture, with its neo-Confucian emphasis on filial piety and harmony, would prevent violent class conflict. Still, the state instituted increasingly harsh restrictions on political speech and organizations in the context of popular protests in the early twentieth century, culminating in the promulgation of the 1925 Peace Preservation Law used to imprison Communists and anti-colonial activists (Ward 2019).

The 1923 earthquake destroyed large sections of Tokyo and Yokohama but boosted efforts of city planners in Tokyo to promote urban regulation of housing density and other matters, a process that had already begun with the comprehensive City Planning Law of 1919. The profession of urban planning flourished over the next decade, encouraged by Home Minister Gotō Shimpei (1857–1929), who had been Tokyo's mayor at the time of the earthquake and was promoted to home minister the next day to manage the crisis. The Dōjunkai Foundation, set up to collect donations for victims of the earthquake, invested in mid-rise worker housing built with reinforced concrete, although on a small scale (Sorensen 2002: 109–33).

Sorensen argues that, despite the impressive achievements of Meiji and post-Meiji urban planners, the Japanese public played a relatively minor and indirect role in urban policy compared to residents of cities in Western Europe and the United States. He attributes this in part to the legacy of urban life in the Tokugawa era (1603–1868): "The fragmented spatial, social and administrative structure of cities in the Tokugawa period has had deep ramifications. It was first and foremost an extremely effective means of social control, as it divided the commoner population into manageable blocks, each of which was run in the image of a family unit, as were the rural villages on which the system was based" (Sorensen 2002: 37). Cohesive, self-managing neighborhoods segregated by status tended to obstruct broader identification with the city. Imperial Japanese planners and officials preferred to keep the focus of patriotic education on the emperor, the country, and the family, not on cities. Japanese cities grew rapidly in the early twentieth century, but their residents harbored "consistently low expectations of local governments" (Sorensen 2002: 38).

Still, Louise Young (2013) argues, many Japanese citizens developed new conceptions of cities in the 1920s. Tokyo was seen as the driver of modernity, while provincial cities were thought to retain more connections to the past, even as they were drawn into Tokyo-led national development. Japanese writers who had relocated to the capital – the center of culture and publishing – depicted their provincial hometowns nostalgically, emphasizing their humble place in the urban hierarchy. Young shows, however, that creativity and entrepreneurship were as common in provincial cities as they were in Tokyo and Osaka. The consciousness of being part of a particular urban community was promoted by such events as a public haiku-writing event in Kanazawa and the publication of a history of Niigata that emphasized the special resilience of its people due to its location in "snow country" (Young 2013: 81, 162).

The Great Depression hit newly industrialized Japan hard in the 1930s, leading to a backlash against liberal politics and a rise in militaristic nationalism. Technocratic urban planners were caught up in the changing cultural mood, as their cosmopolitan connections with planners around the world were questioned. Still, there was plenty of work for them, given the expansion of the Japanese empire. Gotō Shimpei himself, a specialist in public health, had developed the public infrastructure and policing system in Japanese Taiwan as governor earlier in his career.

The Meiji state laid the foundations of empire by centralizing control over islands around its core, including Hokkaido in the north and the Ryukyus to the south, and then extending its influence to Korea, Taiwan, and Manchuria. By 1910, it was busy building cities in all these territories (Figure 3). In the first two decades of the twentieth century, the Japanese claimed to be following the example of European and American imperialism for the good of the "backward" peoples they ruled. With the rise of anti-colonial movements, though, they increasingly characterized their actions as "protecting" Asians from Western imperialism. Scholars continue to debate how twentieth-century Japanese imperialism was distinctive (Booth and Deng 2019). From the point of view of urban history, though, the similarities between it and the European and American versions are obvious: Japanese officials took the leading roles in city planning, managed infrastructure to serve a colonial economy that benefited the imperial metropole more than locals, lived in segregated communities, and built effective police forces to keep local opposition in check.

The Japanese put their symbolic stamp on cities in Taiwan, Korea, and Manchuria, as did the European powers and the United States in the cities

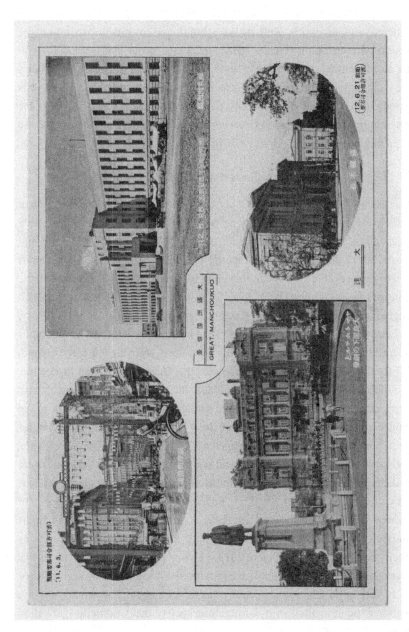

Figure 3 A 1937 postcard featuring Japanese construction in Manchuria. Source: Lafayette College East Asian Collection. https://ldr.lafayette.edu/concern/images/x920fx57q

they controlled. It was easier for planners to operate there – seizing land and redesigning street plans – than it was in the home country (Hein 2003). Trade between "mainland Japan" and the new territories flowed through the modernized ports of Busan and Jilong (Dawley 2019). Both Taipei and Seoul were recentered around plazas with massive buildings constructed to house the Japanese administration (Henry 2014). In Seoul, which had served for 600 years as the capital of the Korean Joseon kingdom, the Japanese governor's office – the biggest building in East Asia when it was constructed in 1926 – was plopped down in the middle of Seoul's palace district, deliberately blocking the geomantic (*pungsu*; *fengshui* in Chinese) energy associated with the site in the Korean planning tradition (Grunow 2016).

3.3 Cities and Urban Governance in Fragmented China

In the case of China, the modern city concept was introduced in an environment in which hundreds of cities had long been embedded in a relatively stable socioeconomic and institutional order (Rowe 2013; Lincoln 2021; Wu and Gaubatz 2021). In China's long imperial era (221 BCE–1911 CE), statecraft aimed to maintain the stability of the realm by encouraging balance among the regions of the vast empire (Pomeranz 1993). Although the coastal areas around Shanghai and Guangzhou were the most prosperous parts of the country, provincial capitals and other administrative centers provided urban amenities that, until the advent of the modern city, were fairly equivalent across the land.

By the mid-nineteenth century, though, the Qing empire was in decline. Rapid population growth had undermined its system of governance, with deleterious effects on infrastructure and social order. Defeat by Britain in the Opium Wars led to the establishment of Hong Kong and the treaty-port concessions, which soon acquired the attributes of the modern city. Chinese residents and visitors compared the technological and other innovations they saw there with the rather dilapidated state of Chinese cities and began to associate modern cities with national strength. By 1900, advocates of urban reform had begun to introduce elements of the modern city in provincial capitals, sometimes employing Japanese advisers with experience in adapting European practices in their own country (Stapleton 2013). Urban reformers tended to justify innovations like professional police and rules about sanitation by arguing they were of service to Chinese statecraft – useful techniques that would help the government achieve the sort of harmonious society that Confucius had called for more than 2,000 years earlier.

While officialdom was trying to absorb elements of the modern city idea into Chinese tradition, though, the lively publishing industry that flourished in foreign-controlled Shanghai presented Chinese with novel conceptions of the world and the role of cities as centers of culture and change. The *Dianshizhai Pictorial*, for example, carried stories from foreign periodicals paired with illustrations by Chinese artists (Ye 2003). In 1889, one such artist crafted an image that belonged to the city of the future: a multistoried building featuring Chinese-style pillars and roofline, with elevators hanging off the side, accompanying a description of a design for a twenty-eight-story building patented (but never built) by Minneapolis's Leroy Buffington in 1888 (Figure 4). In general, the material aspects of modern cities as presented in such sources and as experienced in the treaty ports appealed strongly to Chinese city people. However, foreign ideas about hygiene and attacks on Chinese medicine were not as universally acceptable, as Ruth Rogaski (2004) shows in her study of treaty-port Tianjin.

In Meiji and post-Meiji Japan, a strong, centralized state presided over rapid industrialization and urban modernization but kept municipal government on a tight leash and limited residents' ability to play a role in the management of their cities. In China, on the other hand, effective central control collapsed in the early twentieth century with the 1911 fall of the Qing empire. Until the 1950s, despite the existence of a Republic of China that claimed sovereignty over all of the former territory of the Qing, militarists competed for control, effectively fragmenting the country. During the 1930s, the Nationalist Party of Chiang Kai-shek managed to extend its authority over much of China; it promoted the idea of the modern city and began construction of a capital in Nanjing. War with Japan cut that short in 1937. Throughout the first half of the twentieth century, warfare and famine led to insecurity and much population movement, under-cutting the efforts of urban governments to transform cities and weakening urban communities (Stapleton 2013).

The fragmented nature of the Chinese state between 1911 and the 1930s served in some ways to promote urban development because the central government was unable to control the actions of regional militarists, who tended to regard visually impressive cities as critical to establishing their legitimacy as modern political leaders. They thus kept a close watch on developments elsewhere in China. In terms of roads, buildings, public utilities, sanitary regulations, and uniformed police, most provincial capitals and other major cities acquired the trappings of the modern city in the 1920s and 1930s but often without the resources or job opportunities that modern industry would have provided (Stapleton 2022). The result was a growing gap in material life both between city and countryside and between rich and poor within the cities. This gap would feed into the radical critiques of the modern city that emerged in the 1930s.

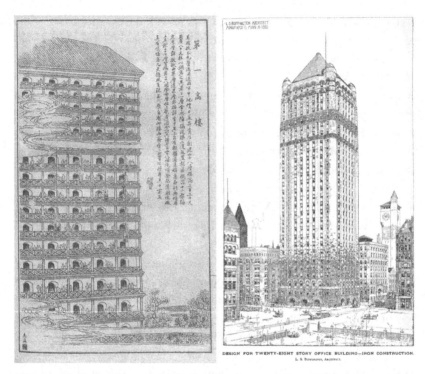

Figure 4 Left: A Chinese artist's imaginative rendering of the twenty-eight-story "Cloudscraper," a building design patented in 1888 by Leroy Buffington. The Chinese text in the image describes features of the building, probably translated from an English-language news report that included no image of the design. Source: *Dianshizhai huabao* (Shanghai) (ca. 1889). Digitized by Bayerische Staats-bibliothek, München, URN:nbn:de:bvb:12-bsb00075645-2, scan 64 of 842. Right: The image of the building included in an industry publication. Buffington's US patent, #383,170, was approved on May 22, 1888. Source: *The Inland Architect and News Record*, 11 (July 1888)

3.4 Global Business, Technological Change, and International Circulations of Urban Practices

Globe-spanning businesses sold the tools for urban modernization – power generators, tramlines, cranes, elevators, and so on – in non-colonized Asian cities as well as in colonial ones. Clients in non-colonized cities sometimes had more opportunities to comparison shop among vendors, but not always, as foreign powers put pressure on weak regimes to sign contracts with particular companies. British steamship companies dominated the global market for steamship transport for decades, even along the length of China's Yangzi River (Headrick 1988; Reinhardt 2018).

The success of a relatively small number of global corporations in securing the work of supplying and installing equipment for transportation, communication, and industry ensured that the world's modern cities shared similar infrastructure. Standard Oil competed with the Asiatic Petroleum Company, a partnership between Royal Dutch and two other European-based companies, to lead in the distribution and marketing of kerosene and petroleum. Each financed storage and canning facilities near many Chinese cities on land that Chinese agents bought or leased, since foreign companies were not allowed to acquire land outside the treaty ports before the 1910s. Standard Oil maintained a fleet of tankers capable of traveling up China's inland rivers (Cochran 2000).

Japanese companies imported locomotives, power looms, and other such equipment from Europe and the United States in the last three decades of the nineteenth century, but they soon began to export their own advanced technological products to China and other parts of Asia (Ericson 1996, Cochran 2000). Particularly during and after WWI, Japanese factories proliferated in China's treaty ports and in Korea, Manchuria, and Taiwan, and Japanese firms dominated the market for some technologies in China (Remer 1933; Yang 2010). The banks that financed industrial ventures often formed consortia across national borders. Japanese companies and the government itself raised capital in London and New York until Japan's 1931 invasion of Manchuria spooked Western financiers (Hausman, Hertner, and Wilkins 2008). The spread of industry around East Asia was uneven but contributed greatly to the adoption of new technologies like macadamized roads. Regional militarists in China wanted to make their urban headquarters "industry-ready" even as they found it difficult to entice investors. They employed experts in urban administration trained in Japan, Europe, and the United States to overhaul their taxation schemes and plan street-widening campaigns (Stapleton 2022).

In addition to the spread of technologies and standards promoted by multinational corporations like Standard Oil, cities were affected by the global circulation of urban visions and administrative techniques via what Pierre-Yves Saunier (2008) calls the transnational municipal movement. Japanese and Chinese municipal administrators and urban scholars participated in this movement, attending international conferences and publishing translations of city regulations and engineering codes in place in the world's major cities. In 1928, China's National Road Building Association published a huge volume of materials on urban development around the world under the title *Complete Book of City Administration* (*Shizheng quanshu*). In addition to regulations in force in cities across China, it covered such topics as the ideal of the Garden City and how to finance urban road construction (Stapleton 2008).

One factor that distinguished the history of urban modernization in China from that in other regions of non-colonized Asia was the strong influence of a network of indigenous merchants who had spent time abroad – in colonial cities in Southeast Asia and in Australia – and returned to invest in their home country. Such "overseas Chinese" used business experience and capital acquired in cities like Singapore and Melbourne to build department stores and housing developments in Shanghai, Guangzhou, and other Chinese cities. An especially notable example is Xiamen (Amoy) in southeastern Fujian Province, which sent many native sons out to find their way in the wider world. Some of the more prosperous returned to contribute to the city's development, including Chen Jiageng (Tan Kah Kee, 1874–1961), who made a fortune in rubber and industrial ventures in Singapore and then returned to found Xiamen University (Cook 2011). The Chinese diaspora's influence in urban development in modern China, although not as well documented, was no doubt much more extensive than the more visible impact of the Sephardic Jewish diasporic families of Sassoon and Hardoon, who built hotels and other businesses in British-dominated Asian cities, including Bombay, Hong Kong, and Shanghai (Chung 2019).

3.5 Modern City Life and Popular Culture in Non-colonized Asia

By the 1920s, the middle class in East Asian cities was expanding rapidly. Louise Young (2013: 195–96) argues that, despite their limited role in urban governance, well-off residents of Japanese cities recognized that "what was good for the city was good for the middle class . . . . 'The city' became a site of intense engagement around future prospects: looking forward with an eye to creating opportunities, channeling resources, directing the course of future development."

In China, the urban middle classes indulged in high hopes for a prosperous urban future too, but they did so in the midst of appalling social crisis. Rural insecurity across much of China in the 1920s and 1930s impelled migration to cities without enough employment opportunities to absorb all the newcomers. Shantytowns and beggars proliferated, especially in coastal treaty ports and provincial capitals. Eventually, the leaders of the Communist movement recruited followers by highlighting the serious inequality visible on the streets of Shanghai and other cities (see Section 4.3). But, among the middle class, supporters of capitalist development and moderate urban reform were much more numerous than Communists until the eve of the Communist victory in 1949.

In the decades before WWII, popular culture in non-colonized Asian cities in many ways resembled that in colonized Asian cities and in cities around the world. Cinemas, dance halls, racetracks, and other new types of entertainment began supplanting older forms of theater and storytelling. Department stores offered opportunities to window shop and people watch, as well as satisfying consumer desires piqued by modern advertising in the daily papers. Whereas in colonies, and especially in diverse colonial cities like Singapore, the middle class tended to adopt the colonizer's language as a status marker and lingua franca, in Japan and China modern popular culture flourished in the "national language," standardized forms of spoken Japanese and Chinese promoted in schools and via radio and film. Command of the national language took a long time to spread beyond the capital cities, however (Lee 1996; Tam 2020).

New features of Japanese and Chinese cities in the 1920s were the so-called modern girls and new women: educated urban women not confined to the paternal home and its strict rules (Wang 1999). Although historians have traced the rise in the 1920s of new images of the modern girl around the world (Weinbaum et al. 2008; Lewis 2016), it was particularly striking in East Asia. Young (2013: 230) points out that, "in the iconography of interwar Japan, women emerged as the quintessential symbol of modern life." The modern girl depicted in magazines, fiction, and film – lively, fashionable, athletic, independent-minded, and consumeristic – captured imaginations across East Asia (Edwards 2020). Far rarer in real life than in the media, the modern girl was both celebrated and reviled. In film and newspaper stories, she often met a tragic end, her love affairs leading to murder or suicide (Dong 2008; Goodman 2021).

The prominence of images of new women and modern girls in East Asia is linked to the rapid growth of the media and consumerism in its booming cities. Middle-class women took charge of furnishing and provisioning their house-holds and displayed their status in their clothing and recreational choices (LaCouture 2021). On the other hand, sexy depictions of modern girls helped sell cigarettes and other products marketed to men (Gerth 2003). A conservative backlash against the increasingly public role of women certainly existed in East Asian cities. In China, however, it was much stronger in inland cities than on the coast. In many colonial cities, the attacks on women in public were framed in religious and/or anti-Western terms, forms of discourse that were more muted in East Asia.

Debate about sex work flourished across Asia in the context of transnational elite concerns about morality and public order. Older practices and cultural perspectives on sex work were transformed in the context of economic change and mass migration, which promoted the commercialization of sexual services (Garon 1997; Hershatter 1997; Huffman 2018).

The housing that developed in new industrial cities in East Asia contributed in some ways to promotion of new cultural forms. Young women constituted the majority of workers in textile mills in Osaka and Shanghai. For them, dormitory life could be oppressive, but it also offered unprecedented opportunities to form friendships with peers from different regions. Free time, while limited, could be spent window shopping or taking advantage of literacy classes offered by groups such as the Young Women's Christian Association (YWCA) and Communist student associations (Honig 1986; Tsurumi 1990). In the case of working-class families, Hanchao Lu makes a strong case that, even in crowded Shanghai, life in the back lanes did not differ much from village life. Shanghai attracted hundreds of thousands of rural migrants in the decades after 1890, but many settled in neighborhoods where relatives and friends were already established. Neighbors met frequently in communal spaces, quarreling with and helping each other as they had in the countryside (Lu 1999).

4 Asian-Based Critiques of City-Centered Development

The modern city as a concept and material phenomenon gained widespread support in Asia. It also became a target for many activists, who associated it with all that was wrong with colonialism, industrialization, and the modern world in general. The most visible critics of city-centered development in Asia, however, took full advantage of the technologies and practices associated with the modern city – publishing their critiques in city-based newspapers and periodicals, traveling from city to city via railroad and steamship, recruiting supporters at urban schools and religious centers, holding mass rallies in public squares, and sometimes assassinating political figures in city streets. By the late nineteenth century, it had become almost impossible to avoid participating in urban life, as James Scott (2009) argues upland Southeast Asian people had managed to do for centuries after their ancestors fled the expanding Chinese empire. Some critics of modern city-centered development tried to shift the focus of social and capital investment from cities to towns and villages. Others attacked the inequities they saw in urban-based capitalist development and presented alternative visions of socialist cities as workers' paradises.

Secular political organizations and religious movements engaged in debates about the benefits and costs associated with modern cities and the transformations they had begun to make in the hinterland. Two individuals stand out for articulating particularly powerful critiques of the modern city concept as introduced in Asia in the years around 1900: Mohandas K. Gandhi and Mao Zedong. The ideologies and activism of Gandhi and Mao shaped thinking about cities and modern life throughout Asia and the world in the middle decades of the twentieth century. After surveying the activities of a range of critics of the modern city, this section examines the movements launched by Gandhi and Mao (for another comparison of Gandhi and Mao on the city, see Ren 2020: chapter 2). The section ends with a brief discussion of some significant impacts of WWII on Asian cities and on thinking about cities.

4.1 The Coevolution of Cities, Religion, and Nationalism in Asia

Modern cities emerged in Asia in a context of competing transnational religious movements, all struggling to define their relationships to the rapidly changing world (van der Veer 2014). American Protestant mission efforts, in particular, surged beginning in the 1890s. The Young Men's Christian Association (the YMCA or the Y) played a significant role in shaping ideas about cities, having developed its own vision of modern urban living, with an emphasis on education, sports, and hygiene. Americans established YMCAs and YWCAs in Asian cities to share this vision, hoping it would lead to the spread of Christianity. A recent volume on the global work of the YMCA credits it with spreading a "Gospel of Modernity" and argues that it should be considered "one of the first international nongovernmental organizations ... effectively pushing a modernization agenda all over the world" (Fischer-Tiné, Huebner, and Tyrrell 2020: 6, 3).

The reception accorded to YMCAs and YWCAs, and Protestant missions in general, varied according to the context into which they were introduced. The French and Dutch did not welcome American Protestant proselytizing in their colonies. American occupation of the Philippines opened that land up to the institution, however; its target audience there consisted mostly of Catholics. The YMCA in the Philippines helped shape popular culture, particularly competitive sports. British colonial officials feared stirring up religious tensions and rebellion, and many were ambivalent about the growth of missionary activities in the empire. But WWI created a demand for the services of the YMCA among the troops, and the Y expanded its work in South Asia after the war, with American backing (Fischer-Tiné, Huebner, and Tyrrell 2020). In Japan, the YMCA grew rapidly until the 1920s. Some former samurai saw Christianity as part of the key to national strength and welcomed the establishment of YMCA branches in Japanese cities. But Jon Davidann (1998) shows that they demanded local control of the YMCA institution almost immediately, leading to conflict with YMCA leadership in the United States.

The impact of the YMCA on conceptions of urban life in Asia was strongest in China, where a weak central government and loosely organized religious communities allowed it to play a more active role in social life. Sidney Gamble, a YMCA secretary in Beijing, carried out and publicized surveys of poverty in the city (Chen 2012). YMCAs in cities across the country sponsored lectures on science and democracy. YMCA leaders also promoted urban development. Wang Zhengting (C. T. Wang), president of the National Road Building Association – publisher of the *Complete Book of Urban Administration* cited in Section 3 – had been the first Chinese general secretary of the YMCA in China (serving 1913–1918) and before that a YMCA secretary in Japan, working primarily among the large Chinese student population (Xing 1996).

The association of some forms of Protestant Christianity, such as the YMCA and YWCA, with the modern city and with "new women" produced a variety of reactions across Asia. In India, "local religious groups, driven by the fear of an impending wave of conversions to Christianity, created their own clones of the Y outfits, including the Young Man's Hindu Association, the Young Man's Buddhist Association, and the Young Man's Indian Association" (Fischer-Tiné, Huebner, and Tyrrell 2020: 16). Other religious leaders explicitly criticized the phenomenon of the modern city, including its liberal culture. Gandhi's anti-urbanism, discussed below, is the most famous, but such criticism took many forms, including among some Asian YMCA leaders. In southern India, the YMCA emphasized "rural reconstruction" among communities of converts – mostly Dalits – rather than urban work, setting up rural cooperatives, microfinance systems, and agricultural extension services in the 1910s and 1920s (Fischer-Tiné 2018; Tyrrell 2020: 146).

In Japan, the speed of industrialization and urbanization during the Meiji era produced ambivalence and hostility in addition to pride. Carol Gluck (1985: 178) argues that it had been common since at least the early eighteenth century for Japanese elites to associate the countryside with the golden past and the cities with "a less congenial present." This sort of juxtaposition became increasingly prominent in the early twentieth century with the rise of complaints about "city fever" – a malady associated with crass materialism and idleness that caused young people to flock to towns, which commentators feared would be carried back to infect the villages (Gluck 1985: 159–62). Voices inside and outside the Japanese state promoted the cult of the emperor, a newly codified Shintō religion, and rural life as fundamental parts of Japan's national identity.

Particularly after WWI, many Japanese agrarian activists argued that "farming was essential to the unique spiritual qualities of the Japanese people" (Havens 1974: 296). Others rejected the growing nationalistic identification of the village as the moral core of Japan, arguing that farming communities had universal human value because they offered an alternative to the exploitative capitalism that had produced the Great Depression (Vlastos 1998). Modern cities, they believed, existed only to exploit the countryside. In a journal founded by agrarian utopians, Yamakawa Tokio characterized the modern city as "a monstrous three-legged idol, stained crimson with the blood of farmers" (Vlastos 1998: 89).

The coevolution of religion, nationalism, and cities is particularly interesting and complex in Korea. In the decades after 1400, deeply committed to neo-Confucianism, officials of the Joseon state had constructed its capital, Seoul, at a particularly sacred site in geomantic terms. They banned Buddhist temples from the city and discouraged the practice of non-Confucian religions in other ways, although not entirely successfully (Walraven 2000). Under the influence of Japan, which incorporated the peninsula into its empire in 1910, Buddhist institutions were welcomed back to Seoul and other cities. The Japanese built Shintō shrines there also. Meanwhile, Protestant missionaries established churches that appealed to Koreans, including many who were unhappy with Japanese rule. The newly urban Buddhist centers tended to cooperate closely with the Japanese regime, emulating the social service practices that the Christian churches had pioneered in Korea (Nathan 2018). Whereas on the Japanese mainland many religious leaders sympathized with and supported the agrarian movement, such figures in Korea tended to ally themselves with the colonial Japanese city-centered modernization project. Beginning in the mid-1920s, some indigenous Christians and other religious activists worked to establish Danish-style rural cooperatives in the Korean countryside in an attempt to promote what they saw as a more desirable "agrarian-pastoral vision of the nation" (Park 2014: 118).

In Muslim communities in South and Southeast Asia, many of which were urban, there was considerable interest in Japan's Meiji-era development. As Japan emerged as a great power with its victory over Russia in 1905, many Muslims began to see it as a possible ally against European imperialists and as a model. Japan's successful construction of a strong military, industry, and technologically advanced cities showed Muslim reformers that a non-Christian nation could modernize while preserving what the Japanese referred to as their "national essence" (*kokusui*), a concept almost as amorphous as "tradition." Some Muslim activists around the world even hoped that the Japanese would convert en masse to Islam (Laffan 2003: 162–65). In the 1920s and 1930s, the Japanese government promoted the idea that Japan was a friend to the world's Muslims (Aydin 2007). It even sponsored tours of Mecca for groups of Asian Muslims. After 1941, when that was no longer possible, Japanese officers considered promoting Japanese-occupied Singapore as the worldwide center of Islam, a new Mecca, although nothing came of that idea (Lewis and Wigen 1997: 72).

Just as the modern city idea reached its height of popularity among Asian elites in the early twentieth century, a growing perception of "rural crisis" emerged in the public consciousness, as the effects of global trade and economic instability disrupted life everywhere. The rural reconstruction work launched by the YMCA in southern India in the 1920s is one manifestation of this. It influenced a similar project in China that began slightly later, led by the YMCA veteran James Yen (Yang Yanchu), who established a model community in eastern China's Ding County (Hayford 1990). These projects criticized what was considered an overemphasis on urban investment. For the most part, though, advocates of rural reconstruction accepted the developmental approach promoted by urban reformers. To them, the weakness of the modern city concept was that its allure obscured the critical contributions of rural areas to the well-being of the broader society, including cities, leading to the neglect of villages and towns.

Over the course of the early twentieth century, colonial and national governments in Asia also began to fear the consequences of the uneven geographic spread of development. Rural poverty led to migration to cities and the growth of dense informal settlements on their peripheries: the dreaded slums. Such places were not only bad for government reputations; they were thought to nourish radical political movements. In India and China, officials launched their own rural development programs and monitored and/or co-opted those started by nongovernmental organizations like the YMCA, which needed official approval to function (Merkel-Hess 2016).

By the 1920s, secular international organizations had also begun to direct attention to increasingly visible rural problems, such as health and economic sustainability. The Rockefeller Foundation expanded its activities across rural Asia, promoting modern medicine and public health (Amrith 2014). The League of Nations sent teams of economic advisers to member countries that requested them (Hell 2010; Zanasi 2013). Such technical missions increased during the Great Depression of the 1930s, as transnational organizations such as the League of Nations and the Institute for Pacific Relations tried to promote international cooperation and forestall world war (Akami 2002). As with the YMCA, some members of this transnational technocracy were critical of aspects of modern cities, but most prioritized helping the countryside achieve the characteristics associated with the modern city in theory, if not always in practice: sanitary regulation, universal literacy, economic productivity, and technological modernization.

4.2 Gandhi and the City

Mohandas K. Gandhi is the most famous Asian critic of the modern city. He grew up in a small town but went to Bombay as a young man to study. In the early 1890s, he lived in London for two years, studying law, and, after failing to establish himself back in Bombay, spent time in Johannesburg, practicing law and protesting discrimination against the Indian community in South Africa. Those experiences produced a strong antipathy to modern urban life. In a speech to a college economics society in Allahabad in 1916, Gandhi said, "It is not possible to conceive gods inhabiting a land which is made hideous by the smoke and din of mill chimneys and factories and whose roadways are traversed by rushing engines" (Hardiman 2003: 76).

Gandhi harnessed and encouraged a wave of anti-British nationalist sentiment in India in the aftermath of WWI. Like the Japanese agrarian activists, Gandhi believed that Indian life had deteriorated as a consequence of industrialization and urbanization. In 1946, Gandhi used a bloody metaphor, slightly less vivid than the one Yamakawa Tokio had used, to sum up his long-held views on the impact of the modern city on villages:

> I regard the growth of cities as an evil thing, unfortunate for mankind and the world, unfortunate for England and certainly unfortunate for India. The British have exploited India through its cities. The latter have exploited the villages. The blood of the villages is the cement with which the edifice of the cities is built. I want the blood that is today inflating the arteries of the cities to run once again in the blood vessels of the villages. (Gandhi 1946: 226)

His village ideal was based on a spiritual conception of the nation. *Swaraj*, or self-rule, required more than evicting the British: he called on the people of India to cultivate simple lifestyles and handicraft production in largely self-governing and equitable village communities. Touring the country via train and automobile in the 1920s and 1930s, Gandhi asked the crowds that gathered to hear him to reject British cloth as well as the developmentalist attitudes of advocates of the modern city (Jodhka 2002; Guha 2018).

Gandhi's model community resembled the ashrams he had established during his sojourn in South Africa and in India after his return there in 1915. At Sabarmati Ashram on the outskirts of Ahmedabad, all community members spent part of each day farming and spinning cotton, everyone wore clothes made of homespun (*khadi*), drinking alcohol was forbidden, and meals were taken communally (Guha 2018). The strategic location of the ashram – next to, but not in Ahmedabad – allowed him to publicize his experiment in rural living and tap into the wealth of supporters among the city's industrialists (Spodek 2011).

Unlike the Japanese agrarian activists and the YMCA, Gandhi was able to move beyond the creation of small model communities to build a mass movement around his idea of the nation. His approach to political change –

careful surveys of local conditions that revealed abusive rule coupled with nonviolent campaigns of resistance to specific injustices (*satyagraha*) – embarrassed the British government and played an important role in promoting Indian independence. The success and visibility of *satyagraha* initiatives, particularly the famous 1930 Salt March, also ensured that Gandhi's critique of modern life and modern cities reached audiences across Asia and the world.

Gandhi's appeal as an anti-colonial activist was widespread in Asia in the interwar years, but even among Indian nationalists, some objected to aspects of his vision, as well as to his strategy to bring about the end of British rule. Some Bengali elites, among others, objected to what they considered Gandhi's distortion of Hindu beliefs as he tried to unite people of different religions and castes in the anti-British effort (Ghosh 2020). The most prominent Muslim anti-colonial leaders, such as Mohammed Ali Jinnah, distrusted and even feared mass mobilization based on appeals to cultural values associated with the Hindu majority population. Jinnah enjoyed modern urban living and did not think of village life as an ideal to cherish (Guha 2018). In the immediate aftermath of WWI, Gandhi built a strong relationship with Jinnah and other Indian Muslim leaders by persuading the Indian National Congress to support the preservation of the Ottoman Caliphate, the key demand of many pan-Islam activists (Laffan 2003; Aydin 2017). But the dissolution of the caliphate in 1924 removed that common ground. Although a few Muslim Indians remained close to Gandhi, he and the Congress lost influence among India's Muslims when Jinnah became head of the Muslim League in the late 1930s.

Gandhi's other great critic among Indian nationalists, the Dalit activist B. R. Ambedkar, considered Indian village life to be the source of the country's fundamental social problem: the stigmatization of "untouchables," who were not allowed to share in the life of the community but were segregated in each village's "ghetto" (Jodhka 2002: 3350). Ambedkar did not see modern cities as the solution to the problem, though, since segregation and discrimination flourished there, too. He devoted himself to building a legal system that could become a useful tool for a social revolution dedicated to equality for all citizens.

Gandhi's personal commitment to ashram living and *khadi* production certainly made him a compelling figure to readers of news reports about him. It was his political strategy of active, nonviolent resistance, though, that had the greatest influence worldwide in the twentieth century, not his critique of the modern city. The two could be separated. Martin Luther King Jr. famously drew on Gandhi's *satyagraha* approach as he led civil rights protests in the United

States in the 1950s and 1960s. Although Gandhi himself had admired Booker T. Washington's earlier work in building Tuskegee, Alabama, into a thriving Black college and agricultural community, King did not share Washington's and Gandhi's enthusiasm for rural life; he used Gandhian tactics to desegregate cities and their public facilities (Slate 2012). Across Southeast Asia, where the British empire had encouraged the migration of Indian workers, Gandhi was famous primarily as an anti-British nationalist, not as a critic of the modern city. Sometimes, even his commitment to nonviolence was ignored. With Japanese support, Gandhi's former Congress colleague Subhas Chandra Bose recruited Indian men and women across Southeast Asia to join the anti-British Indian National Army in 1943; ironically, one of the divisions was named after Gandhi (Guha 2018: 685).

4.3 Mao and the City

Gandhi was outspoken in his criticism of communism as construed in Leninist theory, which became popular worldwide in the 1920s just as his nationalist movement took off. He particularly disliked its emphasis on violence. Other Asian activists, however, found the Russian Revolution inspirational. Many of them learned about communism from agents of the Comintern – the Communist International – or other enthusiasts based in cities where workers, students, and pilgrims from across Asia gathered: Paris, Tokyo, Guangzhou (Canton), Singapore, and Cairo (Laffan 2003; Goebel 2015; Belogurova 2019).

The most influential Asian Communist, Mao Zedong, spent little time in cities before seizing control of them in 1949. He claimed authority based on his knowledge of Chinese village life and his ability to lead a peasant movement. Many of the other early Chinese Communists thought the revolution would make the quickest progress in Shanghai, China's dominant industrial city. Mao, however, believed that the peasants were the most potent revolutionary force in China in the 1920s and 1930s. City people with any money (the bourgeoisie, in Marxist terms) had been seduced by the material cultural and liberal ideas of imperialist powers. The traditional Marxist vanguard, industrial workers, were too few and too easily suppressed in heavily policed treaty ports such as Shanghai. Mao shared Gandhi's view that imperialists had gained control over the country via the cities and that Chinese "compradores" in the modernizing cities were exploiting the countryside, sharpening rural class conflict (Karl 2010: 25).

Mao became the leader of the Chinese Communist Party a few years after it had been driven out of Shanghai by the Nationalist Party leader Chiang Kaishek in 1927. In a series of rural base areas, Mao and his supporters developed their guerrilla warfare tactics, reorganized communities, and honed their message that rural Chinese needed to rise up under Communist Party leadership to save themselves and the country from imperialism, landlords, and the bourgeoisie. Mao called on the countryside to surround the cities and bring the revolution to them (Murphey 1980: 30–31).

The Japanese invasion of eastern China in 1937 produced a flood of refugees, and many young people chose to travel to the Communist base at Yan'an in northwestern China, attracted by the anti-Japanese reputation the Communists had built via propaganda perhaps even more than deeds (Mitter 2013). Life in Yan'an was as spartan as life in Gandhi's ashrams. The ideology cultivated differed considerably but not completely: both Gandhi and Mao asked young city people to live simply, cultivate selflessness, and learn from the peasants.

Like Lenin (and Gandhi's close friend Jawaharlal Nehru), Mao believed that industrialization would benefit humankind when developed within a socialist system. Mao broke with the Soviet model of development in the late 1950s, however, and we will examine Maoist conceptions of socialist cities in Section 5.4. Here, though, it is important to point out that Mao's critique of the modern city as the product of a partnership between foreign imperialists and domestic elites continued to influence world events even after he settled down in Beijing to transform Chinese cities into socialist spaces in 1949. The Communist movements in Malaya and elsewhere in Southeast Asia in the 1950s and 1960s grew in rural base areas and adopted Mao's rhetoric to attack urban society. Most famously and tragically, the Khmer Rouge leader Pol Pot almost annihilated Cambodia's cities and urban populations in the 1970s as he established what Andrew Mertha (2014: 17) refers to as an "*über*-Maoist regime."

4.4 The Impact of WWII on Cities and on the Idea of the City in Asia

Full-scale war between China and Japan broke out in 1937. That fall, the Chinese Nationalist capital, Nanjing, was abandoned by China's rulers and devastated by the Japanese army, which sought revenge for losses in the earlier battle of Shanghai (Lincoln 2021). After most of China's cities had been bombed and starved for years, the US Air Force flattened many Japanese cities. Museums and monuments in reconstructed Nanjing, Hiroshima, and Nagasaki commemorate the costs of total war on civilian populations.

Aside from the obvious destruction visited on cities across East and Southeast Asia, the war changed cities and ideas about them in many ways. It forced China's government to relocate to Chongqing, in the country's southwest, which experienced significant industrialization for the first time, as well as rapid population growth. Refugees from eastern Chinese cities brought their customs and attitudes with them, challenging local gender norms, for example (Stapleton 2020). After the United States entered the war, Americans cooperated with the British to set up a training center in Calcutta as a staging ground for a joint Chinese-British-American advance into Japanese-occupied Burma. Calcutta received an infusion of American popular culture. The need to keep soldiers and other war-related staff protected and fed, though, contributed to the terrible Bengal famine of 1943–1944, during which some three million people in Calcutta's hinterlands died of starvation. Janam Mukherjee (2015: 6) describes the response of many in Calcutta to the crisis as a "shocking proliferation of local venalities: the hoarding of the middle classes; the cruel expedience of extortionary intermediaries; and the mute complicities of an increasingly callous society at large, increasingly inured to death, becoming increasingly more indifferent, month after month, and then year after year." The dream of the modern city was on its deathbed in Asia during the war.

Japan's takeover of colonial cities in Southeast Asia – Hanoi and Saigon in 1940, then Batavia, Manila, Singapore, Rangoon, Penang, and many others in 1942 – highlighted the weaknesses of the colonial regimes that had ruled them with such confidence. The Japanese appointed local elites to lead new governments, but the relationship between the Japanese military and local populations was always fraught. Gregg Huff (2020: chapter 10) shows that Southeast Asian cities expanded and contracted rapidly during the war, as people balanced their need for food – more available in the cities – and their fear of getting caught up in the war. Tensions between Japanese and locals were particularly intense in Malaya, with its large Chinese communities outraged by events in their homeland. The Japanese had made efforts to win the hearts of Muslim Southeast Asians by emphasizing their respect for the religion. But, in Malaya, they treated Chinese Muslims as Chinese, possible enemy agents or sympathizers (Hammond 2020: 160).

As the Japanese began losing battles in 1943 and 1944, their demands for resources from the territories they controlled increased, and harsh security measures were imposed. As in China, city people across Southeast Asia began slipping away to rural areas to join guerrilla resistance organizations, some Communist, some not. Local military units rose up against the Japanese, sometimes with the encouragement of agents of the former colonial powers (Tarling 2001). But Japanese rule had undermined the legitimacy of European colonial powers, even in their former urban bases. The nationalist uprisings of the postwar years were formed during the war, as guerrilla fighters gained confidence in their capacity to rebuild and use cities to represent their own independent nations.

5 Asian Cities during the Cold War: Decolonization and Development

At the end of the most destructive war in human history, reconstruction was the order of the day for states, organizations, and communities across Asia. The imperial powers among the victors moved to reestablish the status quo ante bellum in their Asian colonies and to reconstruct Japan in a way that would remove any future threat from that quarter. China's Nationalist government hoped that its contributions to the defeat of Japan would give it higher status internationally – the Allies formally relinquished their treaty-port concessions during the war – and allow it to serve as a model for other developing countries (Mitter 2019). Anti-colonial leaders such as Ho Chi Minh, Sukarno, and Aung San resisted the reimposition of European authority and began organizing new nations.

Decolonization – the ousting of imperialist powers and the formation of new nation-states across Asia and Africa – occurred relatively quickly after WWII, although not at all smoothly. The 1947 Partition of British India and the consolidation of independent India, Pakistan, and eventually Bangladesh were accompanied by communal violence, mass migration, and lingering territorial disputes. Pakistan's new capital, Karachi, and cities near the new state borders, such as Lahore and Amritsar in Punjab, felt the effects particularly strongly (Heitzman 2008: 171–72). Cold War rivalry resulted in the partition of other former colonies, accompanied by upheaval in cities and countryside: the Soviet Union and the United States supported mutually hostile regimes that set up competing states and national capitals in Korea, Vietnam, and China.

The Cold War decades were a time of nation-building in Asia. New postwar leaders strove to devise ways to tame formerly colonial and/or cosmopolitan cities and fit them into governance systems quite different from those of the United States and European nations. Postcolonial regimes designed cities to reflect their national aspirations and claim legitimacy locally and globally. Cold War alliances influenced the circulation of ideas about cities and the spread of technologies that shaped them. Economic and security concerns also determined how cities were envisioned and constructed. Leaders and planners on both sides of the Cold War encouraged the construction of new urban settlements to facilitate the extraction of resources and control over restive populations and national territory (Wakeman 2016: chapter 3).

This section provides an overview of the construction of political capitals and other impacts of decolonization and nation-building on cities across Asia (see Map 2). It then explores the influence of American and Soviet developmental

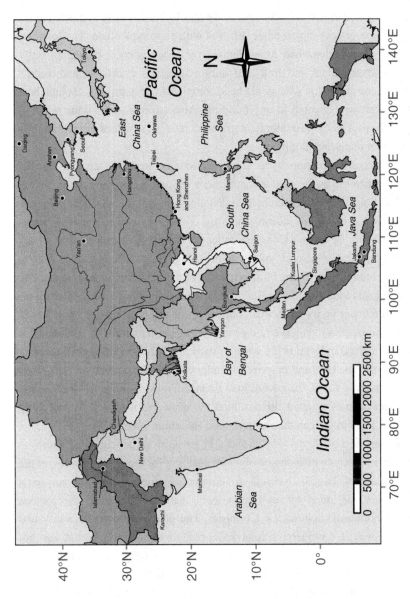

Map 2 Asian cities mentioned in Sections 5 and 6. Map designed by Collin O'Connor, Department of Geography, University at Buffalo, SUNY

and urbanization models in Cold War Asia. It ends with a brief analysis of the Asia-wide influence of the region's ambitious city-state, Singapore.

5.1 Political Capitals in New Nations

The emergence of new nation-states in the late 1940s and early 1950s led to the construction of new capital cities suffused with civic symbolism. The founders of many new nations had long planned for independence, designing flags, shadow governments, and draft constitutions. Postwar exhaustion and conflict imposed constraints on what could be accomplished. It is striking, though, how much effort was devoted to city-building. Also striking is the wide range of approaches taken by postcolonial regimes to reflect the values of the nation in their urban plans and architecture.

Gandhi's assassination by a Hindu nationalist in 1948 left his disciple Jawaharlal Nehru as the predominant leader of India's Congress Party. Nehru, who had long been influenced by socialist ideas, did not share Gandhi's distaste for big government, big industry, and big cities. As independent India's first prime minister, he and his Congress colleagues sought to transform the country without rejecting all aspects of the colonial legacy – reframing much of it to serve the nation. New Delhi, built as the seat of the British colonial government, was designated the national capital. Nehru's government occupied the orientalist buildings put up by the British, but the prime minister himself chose not to live in the ostentatious governor general's palace. Hundreds of thousands of refugees arrived in Delhi in the wake of Partition, setting up their own communities on the outskirts and in spaces abandoned by Muslims who had left. Over the next twenty years, the government financed housing projects for these and other precariously situated citizens, building what it termed New Towns along transport lines in the capital's hinterlands (Heitzman 2008: 173).

The partition of Punjab and the loss of its colonial-era capital, Lahore, to Pakistan necessitated the choice of a new location for the administration of the Indian state of Punjab. Nehru's government decided to build a new city, Chandigarh, designed by an international team that included the famous French modernist architect Le Corbusier. The goal was to create a city that would represent a modern, secular India that respected the past but was not limited by it, particularly by communal divisions of religion and caste. When Nehru first visited the site in 1952, he emphasized the project's significance: "Let it be the first large expression of our creative genius flowering on our newly earned freedom" (quoted in Chalana and Sprague 2013: 200). Whether Chandigarh was a success in planning terms is still debated, but there is no doubt that its construction attracted much attention worldwide.

Pakistan's government settled in Karachi, deciding that Lahore was too close to the border with India. Karachi's municipal corporation was the oldest in India, which benefited the new national capital, as did an influx of experienced administrators among migrants from India. Laurent Gayer (2007: 518) notes, however, that cultural clashes marred the relations between these urban immigrants and the agrarian inhabitants of Sindh, the region surrounding the new capital. In the 1960s, the Pakistani government relocated inland to Islamabad in northern Punjab, newly designed as the "City of the Future" by a leading international urban planner of the era, the Greek architect C. A. Doxiadis. Doxiadis, who had coordinated the reconstruction of Athens with funding from the Marshall Plan, advertised his firm as a purveyor of scientific, non-ideological design that promised to accommodate future growth and aimed to achieve "a blend of indigenous patterns and Western models of progress" (Wakeman 2016: 136). In addition to Pakistan, his firm designed cities in newly independent nations in Southwest Asia and Africa.

Sukarno, president of Indonesia between 1950 and 1965, had trained as an architectural engineer in Bandung under the Dutch. His approach to nation-building was much more capital-centric than Nehru's. Topping his agenda was the reconstruction of Batavia, the old Dutch colonial capital, into a symbol of the nation under a new name: Jakarta. In 1957, Sukarno ignored a master plan for the city that United Nations experts had drafted for municipal authorities in favor of a project of monumental construction that would make Jakarta "an inspiration and beacon to the whole of struggling mankind" (quoted in Kusno 2000: 54). In building Jakarta, Abidin Kusno argues, Sukarno emulated his colonial predecessors in many ways, removing inconvenient settlements – *kampungs*, densely inhabited, low-rise "urban villages" established by rural migrants beginning in the colonial period. The displaced had to fend for themselves to find new homes. As the Indian government had done in Chandigarh, Sukarno used the contemporary global symbolism of international-style architecture to claim a place for Indonesia among leading nations. When Indonesia hosted the Asian Games in 1962, Jakarta's new highways and other construction were highlighted in a set of commemorative stamps (Figure 5). While emphasizing modern infrastructure, Sukarno also drew on old Javanese conceptions of rulership wherein a strong center was thought to attract the loyalty of outlying populations, thereby promoting unity without costly direct intervention beyond the center (Kusno 2000: chapter 2).

In 1965, rising discontent in Jakarta and throughout the country led to unrest and the overthrow of Sukarno. His successor, Suharto, openly appealed to tradition in the built environment, creating a model Indonesian village near Jakarta that emphasized harmony and rural values. Park Chung

Figure 5 Four postage stamps issued in 1962 as part of a set commemorating Indonesia's hosting of the Asian Games and a stamp featuring President Sukarno. Source: Author's collection

Hee, who took control of the Republic of Korea after a military coup in 1962, did something similar in the late 1960s, supporting the creation of a Korean Folk Village (Minsokch'on) so the younger generation of Koreans could learn to appreciate the national heritage as defined by the Park government, even as development ran roughshod over the Korean countryside (Tangherlini 2008). While encouraging their people to respect and emulate rural ancestors and obey the authorities, both Suharto and Park invested in infrastructure to support industrialization – the key, they believed, to national strength. They recognized that adequate housing and basic education were indispensable in that effort, devoting substantial resources to expanding the supply of urban housing and schools. In the 1970s, the World Bank worked closely with the Indonesian government to improve the *kampungs*, which, if not demolished to make way for other projects, had been left out of development initiatives by the Dutch and the postindependence government of Sukarno (Silver 2008; Kwak 2015: 219–21). As former military officers, both Park and Suharto intensified the policing of urban space and emphasized discipline in public life. As the Cold War lingered, many Asian cities became increasingly militarized and securitized by regimes that feared external enemies and internal protest.

In the 1970s and 1980s, South Korea, Taiwan, Singapore, and Hong Kong were often referred to as Newly Industrialized Economies (NIEs) and likened to geese flying in V-formation with Asia's biggest economy, Japan, in the lead. In her study of Seoul, Taipei, and Singapore in that era, Jini Kim Watson (2011: 2) argues that they epitomized "a new model of development in which the city is conceived first and foremost as a production platform – for the production of surplus values, laboring bodies, and national symbols – and less as a site of traditional civic, ceremonial, or economic transactions." Promoting economic development became the main function of cities in the eyes of many Asian elites by the 1970s because economic development had become crucial to the legitimacy of national regimes in an era when the United States and the World Bank dominated international finance.

Taipei, the major city on the island of Taiwan, was ruled by China's Nationalist Party beginning in 1945. Civil war had broken out in China after the Japanese surrender, and the Communist Party conquered most of China by 1949; the Nationalist government relocated to Taiwan, recently recovered from Japan. Pledging to "retake the mainland," the Nationalists considered Taipei a temporary capital and did not invest in monumental construction. Symbolic transformations included the renaming of streets to honor the ideology of Sun Yat-sen, founder of the Republic of China, and to remind residents of the names of mainland cities. Popular resistance to the new regime was crushed, with bloody purges of the Taiwanese elite who objected to the harsh rule of mainlanders. But, after the outbreak of the Korean War, the Nationalists on Taiwan were regarded by American strategists as key allies, and substantial US aid helped Taiwan's economy stabilize and then flourish in the 1970s and 1980s (Allen 2012).

Meanwhile, on the Chinese mainland, the victorious Communists located their central government in Beijing, the capital of the Qing and several earlier dynasties. The imperial palace constructed in the early fifteenth century had become a museum in the 1920s, and the Communists continued to preserve it and other historical sites, using them to illustrate their own Marxist interpretation of the nation's history. The Gate of Heavenly Peace (Tiananmen) gained prominence when the square in front of it was expanded in emulation of Moscow's Red Square (Wu 2005). Shanghai and other industrialized former treaty ports continued to play an important role in the Chinese economy, but their status as symbolic centers decreased – municipal leaders there stressed the need to transform them to "serve the people." The old racecourse at the heart of Shanghai's International Settlement became People's Square, and its clubhouse became a public library. Sex workers entered reeducation facilities aimed at liberating them from what was considered their degradation and making them productive socialist citizens (Hershatter 1997).

Leaders in Asia, as in the rest of the world, sought visibility for their postwar national achievements by hosting international meetings. Nehru welcomed the inaugural Asian Relations Conference to New Delhi in 1947. Bandung, the Javan city where Sukarno had studied architecture in the 1920s, became synonymous with the Non-Aligned Movement after the 1955 Afro-Asian Conference occurred there. U Nu, who succeeded the assassinated Aung San as leader of Burma, invited Theravadin Buddhists from throughout the region to the Sixth Buddhist Council in Rangoon in 1954 (Prakash, Laffan, and Menon 2018). The All-China Women's Federation hosted the Conference of Asian Women in Beijing in 1949, a mere two months after the People's Republic of China (PRC) was founded there (Nasser 2021).

In addition to diplomatic and cultural conferences, high-profile sporting events offered a chance to showcase the nation and its major cities. Sukarno brought the fourth Asian Games to monumental Jakarta (see Figure 5) in 1962 (Kusno 2000: 56). Japan's celebration of nationalism had been muted for more than a decade after the end of WWII; its resurgence was marked in 1964 by Tokyo's hosting of the Olympics. Seoul achieved similar recognition for the Republic of Korea in 1988, and Beijing for China in 2008. By the 1990s, the Cold War had ended and the discourse of "global cities" had taken off, with its focus on an exclusive club of cities that served as central places in a transnational network of economic exchange (see Section 6.1). World expos and conferences of economic elites began to displace sporting events as the key to establishing the prestige of the nation's leading cities and their recognition as "global." In many Asian cities, interest in historic preservation has grown in recent decades, as residents challenge developmentalism and the homogenization of urban space, giving rise to complex political debates over what "heritage" deserves to be conserved and in what forms (Hsiao, Hui, and Peycam 2017).

5.2 Ethnic Diversity and the Postwar Nationalization of Asian Cities

Modern empires mingled populations across Asia. The British and Dutch recruited Chinese and Indian workers to their territories in Southeast Asia. The Soviet Union under Stalin moved Koreans and indigenous Siberians to their Central Asian republics. Decolonization raised the question of the status of such people – even those whose families had migrated several generations earlier – as members of the new nation. Nehru's government, like others in the region, attempted to promote an inclusive concept of national citizenship but without extending it to people who had moved to other parts of Asia in the colonial era. Borders hardened; mobility was restricted. "The world of freely circulating labor was incompatible with that of nation-states" (Prakash, Laffan, and Menon 2018: 7).

Under imperial rule, cities constituted a locus of identity that allowed people to sidestep the complicated question of national identity and imperial belonging.

In their study of nostalgia for colonial Calcutta among Anglo-Indians and Chinese who had grown up there and then moved away, Alison Blunt and Jayani Bonnerjee note that their interviewees "associated the idea of belonging in the city to identifying with a community, which they articulated through personal relationships with family and friends, familiar everyday urban practices and embracing an urban way of life in Calcutta" (Blunt and Bonnerjee 2013: 237). These former Calcutta residents saw their city engulfed by the new nation, a change they could not celebrate.

The collapse of the British empire carried in its wake the so-called princely states; by the end of 1948, Hyderabad's rulers found themselves out of power in the city they had hoped to make a model of Muslim urban modernity (see Section 3.1). After the new Indian federal government seized Hyderabad in a "police action," it installed its own administration there. Taylor Sherman (2015: 176) notes that "unelected military and civilian governments removed Muslims from government employment on the assumption that Muslim employees would act in the interests of the Muslim community, and that those interests were contrary to those of the Indian nation." Urdu, which had been the official language, fell out of use quickly.

All Asian cities, of course, sustained aspects of their distinctive identities in the face of the centralizing and homogenizing efforts of newly emerging nations. Medan, on the northeastern coast of Sumatra, had a population of about half a million in 1954; its people tended to identify more with communities in Singapore and Malaya than they did with residents of faraway Jakarta. Marije Plomp (2012) notes that a Malay-language film industry based in Singapore captured the hearts of the people of Medan, while their own city became known as the "capital of pulp fiction" in the Malay language, appealing to a wide audience across the Straits. Some ambitious writers from Medan decamped to Jakarta to build their careers, but many more remained, resisting the view of nationalists at the heart of the nation that Sumatra was a backwater. Connections with Singapore were attenuated, however, in the mid-1960s, as Indonesia experienced political turmoil and Singapore split with Malaysia. The establishment of national school systems and the promotion of the use of national languages in schools and the media certainly did not completely homogenize urban cultures within Asian countries in the 1950s, but nation-consciousness grew relative to other forms of group identity.

5.3 American Influence and Its Limits

In a 1949 speech, US President Harry Truman observed that global poverty was a problem for the world and a threat to American security (quoted in Mazower

2012: 274–75): "Greater production," he claimed, "is the key to prosperity and peace. And the key to greater production is a wider and more vigorous application of modern scientific and technical knowledge." As interpreted by historian Mark Mazower (2012: 276), American policy in subsequent decades was aimed at "simultaneously dismantling European empires and replacing them with teams of scientific experts, bankers, and technical advisers." The principal model for American-sponsored postwar development was the Tennessee Valley Authority, which combined "agriculture, industry, and power generation, the control of floods and disease, and public health alongside education and urban planning in a single conception" (Mazower 2012: 279).

But, just as with the earlier attempts of imperial powers to promote colonial development, the new postwar world-makers – US government agencies, US-based foundations and corporations, and the (initially, at least) US-dominated United Nations and World Bank – were not consistent in working out their integrated plans and could not control the actions of all stakeholders. They also tended to base their projects on supposed universal laws of development and thus ignored local conditions (Mazower 2012: 285). Nancy Kwak's work on the influence of the American model of private housing and real estate development shows that it appealed widely to elites around the world who saw the value of communities of stable, middle-class homeowners invested in the success of the nation and resistant to communism in "an orderly urban landscape legible to international investors" (Kwak 2015: 51, 89). American efforts spread the ideal of single-family homeownership, but material support for the idea was granted based on American calculations of what would be most beneficial to US interests. Thus, Kwak (2015: 59) points out that Taiwanese dockworkers became the first recipients of American housing assistance in the early 1950s because their work and loyalty were key to the successful defense of the Republic of China on Taiwan, America's ally against the Chinese Communists. Ports and industrial cities, as strategic sites, attracted substantial investment during the Cold War.

Even larger amounts of US aid went to construct housing in South Korea, fighting a hot war against Communist North Korea in the early 1950s and dealing with waves of refugees. The United Nations promoted the construction of simple tamped-earth houses, to the dissatisfaction of South Korean officials, who preferred more advanced materials. Kwak notes that the American-style houses built in South Korea lacked courtyards, an integral and well-used part of most Korean homes (Figure 6). American housing aid to the Republic of Korea continued well after the war ended with an armistice in 1953. Private investors created the American Korea Foundation to work with the US and Korean governments in the area of real estate development, but their limited efforts in Seoul produced houses that proved too expensive for the target buyers and not

Figure 6 Traditional Korean courtyard residences in front of tamped-earth houses built in Seoul in 1953–1954 with support from the United Nations Korea Reconstruction Agency (UNKRA). Source: UNKRA online exhibit S-0526–031-19, United Nations Archives. The photograph is reproduced on the cover of Kwak 2015

well suited to Korean lifestyles. Eventually, the two governments shifted to offering inexpensive financing for home construction by families and private companies, establishing building codes, and publicizing the benefits of modern housing (Kwak 2015: 80–84).

The US postwar influence was widespread in Japan, especially during the Occupation years between 1945 and 1952 (Okinawa was US-administered until 1972 and still houses the largest of many Asian-based US military facilities). Occupation officials and their Japanese partners attempted to address what they saw as the major causes of prewar Japanese militarism via reform of industry and education, land reform, and a new constitution. The city as a concept did not figure prominently in the work of the Occupation, and relatively little of its material effort was devoted to cities. Locals rebuilt the cities pretty much along prewar lines, with dense low-rise neighborhoods, a crazy-quilt street pattern, and multiple commercial centers. Sorensen (2002: 154) notes that, with the approval of Occupation authorities, "the generation of planners who had found work opportunities in the colonies and occupied territories played an important role in the post-war reconstruction projects."

By the late 1960s, and particularly at the height of the US war in Vietnam, many Japanese began to question Japan's dependence on and identification with the United States. Historian Jordan Sand points out that some theorists celebrated the qualities of Japan's cities that had been relatively untouched by American influence: flexibility, heterogeneity, walkability, and liveliness. "As the intimate and accidental came to challenge the monumental and symbolic in urban design thought, Japan seemed to have something unique that distinguished it favorably from the West" (Sand 2013: 32). The tremendous successes of Japanese high-tech companies in the 1970s and 1980s, on the other hand, led others to see Japanese cities as testing grounds for technological innovation including broadband internet, electronic payment systems, earthquake-resistant buildings, and energy-saving construction. Japanese planners began taking leading roles in urban transportation projects across Southeast Asia in the 1970s (Rimmer 1993).

5.4 The Soviet Model of Urban Development in Asia

Because so many Asian activists were inspired by the Russian Revolution, the Soviet path to urbanization sparked interest across Asia beginning in the 1920s. Comintern agents sent around the world to promote revolution shared techniques for organizing workers and keeping newly formed Communist parties secret and safe from the authorities. A steady stream of young people traveled to Moscow to study, witnessing its socialist transformation at first hand. China's first major compilation of articles on urban topics, the 1928 *Complete Book of Urban Administration* (see Section 3.4), included a long essay on Soviet nurseries and their promise to raise children scientifically while freeing mothers to work in industry (Stapleton 2008).

The Soviet Union included a vast amount of Asian territory, and its model of city-building was introduced as part of its central planning process in member states such as Kazakhstan and via cooperative projects in dependent states such as Mongolia. Soviet influence across Asia grew dramatically after WWII, with the formation of Communist regimes in North Korea, China, and Vietnam. Its influence spread, as well, to nonaligned countries, including India, which had an interest in rapid industrialization and were willing to accept some types of Soviet aid. Katherine Zubovich's forthcoming Element on socialist cities analyzes the extent of Soviet influence on city-building in the socialist world. Here, the nature and limits of Russian influence on ideas about cities are discussed briefly in the context of the Chinese case.

The Chinese Communists spent decades building their regime in rural base areas before they captured major Chinese cities in the years after WWII. Without expertise in managing cities, they relied on non-Communist technicians but also began training loyal party members, most of them soldiers, to take over city governments after the founding of the PRC in 1949. James Gao's 2004 study of early 1950s Hangzhou, a wealthy coastal city considered one of China's most beautiful, shows that these soldiers themselves were transformed by urban culture even as they introduced a new sort of discipline. Koji Hirata (2020) notes that the Chinese Communist Party built on the efforts of the Japanese occupation and Nationalist administrators to continue to expand steel production in the northeastern city of Anshan. Nehru was impressed during a visit in 1954.

Mao's government welcomed several thousand Soviet advisers to help with the redesign of cities like Anshan to accommodate large-scale industry and worker housing. Most of China's provincial capitals were allocated new industrial facilities in the First Five-Year Plan (1953–1958), building on the infrastructural developments made there under the Nationalists. As Jeremy Brown (2012) points out, China adopted the Stalinist approach to industrialization: top-down planning oriented around the goal of squeezing resources from the countryside to feed heavy industry in the cities. Groups of experienced workers were relocated from cities on the coast to jump-start the new factories in provincial cities.

The relationship with the Soviet Union soured soon after Stalin's death in 1953, however, and subsequent accounts of early PRC urban development produced in China downplay the Soviet influence. During the Great Leap Forward (GLF), launched in 1958, the Chinese Communists emphasized the decentralization of industry, encouraging regional self-reliance in the production of steel and other materials. The large communes formed during the GLF aimed for economic self-sufficiency and the full employment of all available resources. The new Maoist urban model was Daqing, a city built in the 1960s among newly discovered oil fields. Tens of thousands of workers were transferred there; their wives and other family members who were not employed extracting oil built the city's residential infrastructure, including simple tamped-earth houses dubbed *gandalei* (Figure 7; Hou 2018). The Communist Party urged industrial workers to "Learn from Daqing!" in the 1960s and 1970s. Unlike older cities, it had no monuments, high-rises, or entertainment venues. The emphasis was on productivity, standardization, self-reliance, and simplicity in service to the nation.

In his writing and speeches, Mao famously criticized the urban bias that he saw in modern Chinese history and accused Chinese Communist leaders

Figure 7 *Gandalei* village in Daqing, 1974. Source: Daqing geming weiyuanhu
(1977). *Daqing* (Shanghai: Shanghai renmin chubanshe). The image is
reproduced on the cover of Hou (2018)

themselves of perpetuating it. Before and during the Cultural Revolution, he
instructed young urban people to go to the countryside to "learn from the
peasants," and some seventeen million of them did. But certain policies
adopted with his support undermined Mao's supposed devaluation of cities
in favor of rural communes. Most important was the household registration
(*hukou*) system, which tied urban status to subsidized food, housing, and
social services (Chan 2009). The *hukou* system originated during the GLF
when poor planning and other administrative errors led to famine. To stem the
flood of starving migrants into the cities, the state promulgated *hukou* regulations that made it almost impossible for those without an urban registration
to travel to or live in the cities. In effect, an "urban *hukou*" meant a guarantee
of at least a minimal livelihood, whereas a "rural *hukou*" was a license to
starve in a crisis.

The intensification of hostility with the Soviet Union in the 1960s led to
a recentralization of planning and a geographic shift in the PRC's investments
in industry and urban development. Covell Meyskens (2020) analyzes the
"Third Front" campaign to relocate industrial production to remote, moun-
tainous areas in China's west, where it would be safer from foreign attack.
Although people who already lived in these areas welcomed the investment,

Meyskens (2020: 30) concludes that workers asked to populate the new urban centers generally were not happy: "Upon arriving in the Third Front, many urbanites quickly longed to leave impoverished inland areas and work at state-owned enterprises with extensive welfare provisions in centrally located cities."

Similarly, many of the students sent to live on communes and learn from the peasants grew tired of rural life and disillusioned with the political system that had exiled them from the cities. Mao's attempt to decenter and dismantle the modern city in favor of productive, self-reliant communities like Daqing ultimately withered away after his death in 1976 in what Rhoads Murphey (1980) called "the fading of the Maoist vision." As noted in Section 4.3, the Maoist vision lived on in the late 1970s, in a horribly distorted form, as the Khmer Rouge purged Cambodia of modern cities before being overthrown by the Communist Vietnamese government.

5.5 Singapore as a Pan-Asian Urban Model

The post-Mao Chinese leadership of the 1980s, headed by Deng Xiaoping, did not look to the Soviet Union or the Mao era for guidelines for how to build cities. It looked to Singapore (Calder 2016). Over the course of previous decades, Singapore had emerged as a new model for governments across Asia. Singapore's "brand" – as an efficient, productive, stable order run by a strong state that ensured that its citizens were housed and fed – was the creation of a team of skilled administrators headed by Lee Kuan Yew, the longtime prime minister. Trained as a lawyer in Britain, Lee adroitly navigated the messy politics of decolonization in the British Straits Settlement. After Singapore was expelled from Malaysia in 1965, Lee dominated the city-state's politics as leader of the People's Action Party (PAP), continuing to wield much influence until his death in 2015 (Barr 2019).

Michael Barr (2019: 115) argues that "the PAP government's urbanization plans were ... part of the key to achieving long-term political hegemony and remaking Singapore as a node of modernity." By 1966, Barr notes, public housing accommodated 23 percent of Singapore's population. That percentage grew steadily over subsequent decades; about 90 percent of Singaporeans now live in publicly subsidized high-rise housing (Chua 2011; Kwak 2015). Cheap, efficient public transit was another government priority. The Singapore government targeted investment at industries it considered critical for its economic future. An Economic Development Board recruited international corporations by offering factory sites equipped with excellent infrastructure and promises of well-educated, disciplined workers.

In addition to emphasizing productivity, Lee Kuan Yew was also sensitive to the importance of symbolism in creating the Singapore brand. Commenting on Lee Kuan Yew's 1964 tour of seventeen African capitals, Jini Kim Watson (2011: 180–81) notes that Lee was most struck by those that seemed orderly and not ostentatious, seeing in them a visual promise of competence, social cohesion, and long-range thinking. That's what Singapore aimed to achieve through public construction. In addition, Chua Beng Huat (2017: 33) argues that the government emphasized Singapore's vulnerabilities in the Cold War environment, using them to make demands on the people: "Deviation from the collective effort could potentially be framed as threatening national survival and thus justify calls for state intervention, including political repression." Singapore's successes, Chua notes, have allowed it to present itself as a model of urban and national development that offers an alternative to American and European models. Singapore's role is particularly notable in the context of the emergence of China as an urban nation because it has provided funding and expertise for many urban innovations in contemporary China (Calder 2016).

6 Contemporary Urbanism in Asia and Asian Cities of the Future

In the 1980s, the end of the Cold War contributed to rapid globalization. Economic actors sought out new opportunities around the world, spurred on by consumers and investors in developed regions, as well as by governments, entrepreneurs, and cheap labor in less developed ones. The effects of the economic globalization of recent decades on the world's cities have prompted new conceptualizations of cities and urbanization that attempt to incorporate a global perspective. One theoretical approach focuses on the phenomenon of the "global city," embodied in major business centers that serve as bases for the operations of global finance capitalism. Another highlights an ongoing process of "planetary urbanization," in which all of the earth's surface is reorganized according to its relationship to cities and urban networks.

Both of these bodies of theory incorporate Asian urbanism in their research frameworks and conceptualizations. Their development, however, has been centered in universities in North America and Western Europe. Many scholars and activists most concerned with other parts of the world have called for theories of the urban that center on conditions and knowledge produced in the "Global South," a concept that has largely supplanted the older term "Third World." The Global South encompasses communities that experienced modern colonization and its lasting postcolonial economic and cultural effects. In particular, scholars of India and parts of Southeast Asia have joined colleagues who study Africa and Latin America to highlight the concept of "informality" as a critical characteristic of cities in the Global South, as well as to analyze the effects of urban environmental crises as postcolonial legacies.

Although China also suffered the effects of modern imperialism and thus is generally included in conceptions of the Global South, its recent urban history stands out from that in other parts of the Global South. The government of the PRC conceives of cities very differently than do Western liberal or leftist and Global South theorists. Urbanization is seen as a comprehensive process that should extend to every part of the country, tying it together to promote economic growth and social stability. Given the growing international influence of the PRC in the contemporary world, the model of urbanism promoted by the Chinese Communist Party, with its emphasis on security and its firm limits on the autonomy of urban communities, promises to be increasingly influential in Asia and beyond.

6.1 Global Cities and Planetary Urbanism

As noted in Section 5, the early Cold War years saw the consolidation of an international system that featured new nation-states in Asia and other parts of the formerly colonized world. Their autonomy was compromised, certainly, by the constraints of Cold War geopolitics. But, in terms of their domestic political economy, national governments tended to gather up resources and use them to shape cities and urban life in support of national prestige and industrialization. In the 1970s and 1980s, many scholars argue, the economic decision-making of the nation-state began to be overshadowed by that of multinational corporations and other agents of global capitalism. Social scientists have analyzed the impact of this shift on cities.

Sociologist Saskia Sassen famously identified a set of what she called global cities – New York, London, and Tokyo – that serve as centers of international finance and service industries that help multinational corporations manage widely dispersed production. Her 1991 book on this phenomenon highlighted the tensions within global cities as well as their economic dominance. Sassen (1991: 331) pointed out that Japanese planners sought to address the problem of high housing costs and long commutes by linking Tokyo's urban core via high-speed rail to adjacent regions and cities, creating a megacity. Osaka's post-WWI mayor, Seki Hajime, would not have found this idea too surprising, since he advocated for streetcars and garden suburbs for the city's workers (see Section 3.2). Sassen observed, however, that the scale of municipal Tokyo posed huge new challenges for urban governance that have not been resolved. Still, Tokyo's experience and wealth allowed companies and consultants based there to have an outsized influence on urban construction in cities across Southeast Asia just a few decades after the end of WWII – a striking sign of the ascendence of global capital and Tokyo's centrality in its spread (Silver 2008: chapter 6; Zhao 2019).

The idea of the global city and the widespread recognition of the importance of financial and managerial services in the globalized economy shape the way major Asian cities other than Tokyo attempt to market themselves. Singapore and Hong Kong moved away from manufacturing in the 1980s and 1990s to highlight their transportation and communication facilities, their stable financial institutions, their outstanding educational systems, and the intimate knowledge of the growing Chinese economy among their business communities (Calder 2016; Hamilton 2021). More recently, the competition for prominence among cities in Asia has been influenced by the idea that successful cities must welcome the "creative classes" – an idea promoted by the work of urbanist Richard Florida (2002). One result is increasing investment by Asian governments, national and municipal, in entertainment districts and other amenities thought to be appealing to dynamic and mobile young "thought leaders" (Sasaki 2010; Kim 2017).

Urban theorists Neil Brenner and Christian Schmid (2014) promote a broad perspective on cities around the concept of planetary urbanization. They note that contemporary urbanization is not characterized, as in older conceptions of the modern city, by clear political jurisdictions and city services that extend only to the outskirts of town. Rather, they argue, "urbanization is a process of continual sociospatial transformation, a relentless 'churning' of settlement types and morphologies that encompasses entire territories and not only isolated 'points' or 'zones' within them" (p. 750). In critiquing "territorialist and settlement-based understandings of cityness," Brenner and Schmid emphasize the global interconnectedness of socioeconomic processes around the world, which they think has been overlooked in urban studies. Regional diversity and its historical underpinnings must be studied within a broader framework of planetary scope, they insist.

Contemporary urban theory is stimulating and ambitious, but perhaps not ambitious enough. It often neglects urban history. Although Sassen's work is sensitive to the different historical trajectories of the global cities she examines – she contrasts Tokyo and New York as well as compares them – much of the theorization about the transformation of cities and urban networks resulting from globalization does not engage deeply with history. The "deterritorialization" that scholars associate with the current age of capitalism (Cox 2013) has tended to obscure the distinctiveness of regional developments of the past and divert the attention of many social scientists away from historical work. Brennan and Schmid (2014: 749) quote a fellow urban theorist, Jennifer Robinson, on the need to foster a "'rich and fragmented array of ongoing conversations across the world of cities' that will serve to unsettle parochially defined theoretical certainties," but their own work does not feature analyses of how the process of planetary urbanization has been playing out in Asia in particular. Within the field of Global South urban studies, to which Robinson has contributed, however, Asian urban history is critical.

6.2 Asian Cities and the Global South

Geographers who study the world's urban regions by analyzing large data sets have documented striking regional diversity, for example, in environmental vulnerability. Haase et al. (2018: 24) report that "with regard to the value of property and infrastructure assets' exposure to coastal flood risks, a global ranking of megacities includes eight from Asia." Global South theorists seek to explain the distinctive challenges facing cities that developed under colonial and postcolonial regimes, challenges that include the neglect of such cities within most frameworks of urban theory. The focus of Global South urban studies is thus on the experience of urbanization in Asia, Africa, and Latin America. Scholars of India and Southeast Asia, in particular, have played leading roles in this effort.

The great variety of work being done under the rubric of Global South urban studies can be seen in the pages of the *Routledge Handbook of Urbanization in Southeast Asia*, edited by Rita Padawangi (2019), and the *Routledge Handbook on Cities of the Global South*, edited by Susan Parnell and Susan Oldfield (2014). Introducing the section of the latter book that most explicitly addresses urban history, Parnell notes that the scholars whose work is represented in it "highlight how, across the global south, the post-independence failure to fundamentally reconfigure the dysfunctional legacies of colonial housing, planning, and land use management to address the needs of all citizens underpins the complex structural inequities that are the hallmark of contemporary urban problems" (p. 74).

The relationship of many urban dwellers to the inequitable postcolonial city is encapsulated within the Global South literature by the term "informality." A large percentage of residents of cities in the Global South have never enjoyed the formal rights of citizenship in the idealized modern city. Their relationship to the city's official governmental and economic institutions is informal. An "informal settlement," a term that some use in place of "slum," is thus an area of the city where the official government has little sway and that operates according to a logic that is understood locally but is made intentionally opaque to municipal authorities in order to protect the inhabitants from outside interference. Figure 8 reveals the diverse texture of contemporary Chandigarh, the

Figure 8 A photograph of Chandigarh taken on September 2, 2016. Source:
Raman Kumar Insan / EyeEm, courtesy of Getty Images

capital of the Indian state of Punjab discussed in Section 5.1. Places of this
nature thrived in colonial settings and have expanded even more rapidly in
recent decades (Davis 2006).

Liza Weinstein (2014) analyzes the ability of the residents of one such place –
Dharavi in Mumbai – to resist attempts to dispossess them from "some of the
most highly sought-after real estate" in the city (p. 170). She traces the rise of
the community from the colonial era; at that time, British officials and Indian
elites ignored the growing settlement in Bombay's marshy outskirts but profited
from the cheap labor accommodated there. After Indian independence, the
community was targeted by repeated campaigns to upgrade or demolish it,
none of them effective. Weinstein attributes this in part to the fragmented
authority of Indian municipalities as they emerged from the colonial era. Also
critical was determined resistance on the part of residents, who continue to hang
on in Dharavi even in the face of a real estate boom set off by the liberalization
of the Indian economy beginning in the 1990s.

As noted previously, in addition to informality, theorists point to environmental
vulnerability as a characteristic of cities of the Global South. Extreme events such
as hurricanes and drought-induced fires affect cities across the globe, but the
impact on cities with densely packed informal districts is often especially severe.
Slower crises such as rising sea levels threaten coastal megacities; drought and
heat waves cause stress in inland cities. The Sustainable Urban Development
Network of the United Nations created a Cities and Climate Change Initiative in
2008, bringing together urban experts and administrators primarily from Asia and

Africa to work on approaches to managing environmental issues particular to their rapidly urbanizing societies (Simon and Leck 2014).

Some scholars writing within the framework of Global South studies see Asian urbanism as offering potential solutions for urban problems experienced throughout the world. In 2011, Ananya Roy and Aihwa Ong published an edited volume of Asia-focused urban studies under the title *Worlding Cities: Asian Experiments and the Art of Being Global*. In the introduction, Ong argues that the density and liveliness of Asian cities create environments supportive of new ideas about urban possibilities. Still, she points to the persistence of "a kind of psychological vertigo induced in Asian leaders by the distance to be traveled in order to catch up with the development benchmarks and metropolitan ideals established by and in the West" (p. 9). Postcolonial attitudes among elites limit the extent to which popular experimentation in Asian cities can become visible and valued.

Urban theory and visions developed within the Global South framework, in short, are sensitive to Asian history to a much greater degree than urban theory in general. But often the view of history adopted in such scholarship is bounded by the colonial and postcolonial periods. The significance of earlier Asian history to contemporary and future concepts of urbanization and urbanism remains relatively unexplored. In China, though, historical narratives are increasingly representing the era of Euro-American and Japanese domination as an aberration and stressing continuity across the *longue durée*. This new cultural confidence has produced, as William Callahan (2013: 8) puts it, "a shift from locating the future outside China (by figuring China as backward and the West as advanced) to see China itself as the future." Thinking about the nature of cities and the future of urbanization is part of this ongoing reconceptualization project.

6.3 Is a Chinese Model of Urbanization Emerging?

Comparing city politics in India and China, sociologist Xuefei Ren (2020: 20) argues that those countries are near the extreme ends of a continuum between "territorial" approaches to governance – in which a hierarchy of state institutions manage affairs in urban neighborhoods and districts – and "associational" approaches – in which coalitions of organizations and activists push relatively passive municipal offices into action. Whereas India's weak municipal governments are largely a legacy of the colonial era, Ren argues, China's political structure is shaped by a long history of statecraft focused on how to balance central control and local initiative. Geographer Carolyn Cartier (2002: 124) also emphasizes continuity in Chinese statecraft, pointing to the effective use of "scale strategies" to help explain the dynamics of China's urbanization over many centuries: "The scaled administrative system of imperial China worked to stabilize the regions and knit the empire into a coherent whole. That stability, however, was not a static geography of bounded territories but active and highly managed." Cartier (2016) shows that many of these strategies – such as linking the scope of local authority to a city's rank in an adjustable official urban hierarchy – characterize contemporary Chinese administration also.

Over the past twenty years, while drawing from aspects of the Chinese imperial statecraft tradition, the PRC government has initiated a new program of "urban-rural coordination" that, Nick Smith (2021) argues, is speeding up a local version of planetary urbanization. *Hukou* policies adopted in the late 1950s that separated urban and rural populations and that privileged cities (see Section 5.4) are gradually being replaced by policies intended to integrate cities and their hinterlands and spread urban technologies and culture evenly across the breadth of China. The goal, Smith notes in the title of his book, is "the end of villages" as distinct cultural spaces. Rural people, including seminomadic herders in Tibet and Inner Mongolia, have been resettled into dense developments in order to create a "new socialist countryside" (Yeh 2013). Thorough urbanization on a national scale has been presented as the necessary and positive outcome of "scientific" economic development. Smith (2021) shows, though, how both central plans themselves and the attempted depoliticization of the process have been challenged by the maneuvering of local officials and dispossessed farmers. Serious environmental problems continue to grow with the increased pace of urbanization (Wu and Gaubatz 2021: 348).

The Chinese government has powerful tools to shape the narrative about the future of cities and urbanization. It has encouraged cities to celebrate their own histories and cultures in new museums and tourist sites, but such histories need to be framed as contributing to the rise of the Chinese nation, just as their economies contribute to national wealth. The process of integration of all Chinese cities into a political system that emphasizes their service to the nation has been seen most dramatically in recent years in Hong Kong, which became part of the PRC in 1997 after negotiations between the Chinese and British governments. As part of the agreement, Hong Kong was declared a Special Administrative Region under a framework known as "One Country, Two Systems," which allowed the former colony to manage local affairs under its own legal system. With the adoption of a new National Security Law in summer 2020, though, many critics of the government who promoted the idea that Hong Kong should decide its own future have been jailed. Many others have emigrated. Outside observers wonder if Hong Kong is becoming "just another Chinese city."

Of course, Hong Kong, like Singapore (see Section 5.5), has also influenced urbanization in the PRC, via investment, technology transfer, and development models. The extent to which Hong Kong will be transformed by Chinese policy is not yet clear. The PRC government's attempt to establish a new integrated model of national urbanization is aspirational and will be challenged and even ignored – just as with British sanitation regulation in nineteenth-century Singapore or the efforts of post-WWII American housing specialists to promote single-family homeownership around the world. Aihwa Ong (2011: 20) notes that, even in Beijing, where the state hired "starchitect" Rem Koolhaas to design the CCTV Headquarters into what she sees as a "hyperspace of Chinese sovereignty," ordinary city residents subvert the intended message by making jokes about it – dubbing it, among other things, the "giant underpants."

Sociologist Xiangming Chen (2014) argues that China has been more successful than other countries of the Global South at urbanizing while spreading the wealth geographically. This may be due in part to the long history of statecraft that emphasized balanced development as a way to ensure political stability. Likewise, the Chinese government's enthusiastic adoption of advanced surveillance and management techniques such as facial recognition and social credit systems, another way in which it is influencing thinking about urban space around the world (Smart and Curran 2022), is justified by reference to a paternalistic conception of the state grounded in imperial statecraft and socialist ideology. The government's ability to lock down enormous cities during the COVID-19 pandemic has amazed the world even as it has raised concern about the future of civil liberties that were once associated with the modern city.

Chen (2014: 169) notes that global economic processes may not allow the Chinese government to continue to occupy the driver's seat and promote its approach to urbanization: "The Chinese state has created a lot of wealth by building prosperous cities and inserting them into the global economy. But its growing inability to redistribute this wealth and manage the vicissitudes of the global economy has become a current weakness of its earlier strength." Still, Chinese investment in Southeast Asia and Africa may be a pathway by which a "Chinese model" of urbanization will spread. It is surely the case that its influence is growing.

6.4 Concluding Reflections

The idea of the modern city emerged in the context of rapid urbanization spurred by industrialization. Modern cities came to be associated with a cluster of characteristics including public services such as transportation systems and water supply, new forms of entertainment such as cinema, participatory politics, and new opportunities for young men and women to choose their own paths, as well as great inequality, various types of segregation, and uprootedness. Many of the phenomena formerly associated with the modern city have spread beyond what were thought to be its borders. The significance of cities as places and symbols varies widely across the world these days. In the inaugural Element in this series, Richard Harris (2021) makes the case that "cities matter" because of their outsized economic and cultural influence on their surroundings and on the world. But the old image of the modern city that developed in nineteenth-century Europe and spread across Asia is being replaced by new conceptions of urbanization, many originating in Asia.

This Element has focused for the most part on official and elite conceptions of cities. It has passed lightly over the rich history of popular conceptions of cities and urban life in Asia, which have also evolved over the years. Cultural histories of the idea of the city by scholars such as Jini Kim Watson (2011) and community studies such as Liza Weinstein's of Dharavi reveal urban visions shaped by lived experience more than elite projects. The Pakistani journalist Mahim Maher (2018: 353–54), for example, speaks lovingly of the "ugliness" of his hometown, Karachi, and adds "Somehow, I just wanted Karachi to be left alone. When the politicians running the city would talk about 'improving' it and making it like Dubai, I would recoil inside." He acknowledges Karachi's many problems but longs for them to be addressed not by pursuing plans devised by experts but by building a local consensus about what kind of community residents wish to inhabit. Such local visions will continue to challenge and inform globally circulating ideas about the city as long as cities exist.

References

Abu-Lughod, J. (1991). *Before European Hegemony: The World System A.D. 1250 to 1350*. New York: Oxford University Press.

Adas, M. (2014). *Machines as the Measure of Men: Science, Technology, and Ideologies of Western Dominance*. Ithaca: Cornell University Press.

Akami, T. (2002). *Internationalizing the Pacific: The United States, Japan and the Institute of Pacific Relations in War and Peace, 1919–1945*. New York: Routledge.

Allen, J. R. (2012). *Taipei: City of Displacements*. Seattle: University of Washington Press.

Amrith, S. S. (2014). The Internationalization of Health in Southeast Asia. In T. Harper and S. S. Amrith, eds., *Histories of Health in Southeast Asia: Perspectives on the Long Twentieth Century*. Bloomington: Indiana University Press, 161–79.

Andaya, L. Y. (1999). Interactions with the Outside World and Adaptation in Southeast Asian Society, 1500–1800. In N. Tarling, ed., *The Cambridge History of Southeast Asia*, vol. 1, part 2, *From c. 1500 to c. 1800*. Cambridge: Cambridge University Press, 1–57.

Aydin, C. (2007). *The Politics of Anti-Westernism in Asia: Visions of World Order in Pan-Islamic and Pan-Asian Thought*. New York: Columbia University Press.

Aydin, C. (2017). Muslim Asia after Versailles. In U. M. Zachman, ed., *Asia after Versailles: Asian Perspectives on the Paris Peace Conference and the Interwar Order, 1919–33*. Edinburgh: Edinburgh University Press, 55–76.

Barr, M. D. (2019). *Singapore: A Modern History*. London: I.B. Tauris.

Belogurova, A. (2019). *The Nanyang Revolution: The Comintern and Chinese Networks in Southeast Asia, 1890–1957*. Cambridge: Cambridge University Press.

Beverley, E. L. (2011). Colonial Urbanism and South Asian Cities. *Social History* 36(4), 482–97.

Beverley, E. L. (2015). *Hyderabad, British India, and the World: Muslim Networks and Minor Sovereignty, c. 1850–1950*. Cambridge: Cambridge University Press.

Biggs, D. (2010). *Quagmire: Nation-Building and Nature in the Mekong Delta*. Seattle: University of Washington Press.

Blunt, A., and J. Bonnerjee (2013). Home, City and Diaspora: Anglo-Indian and Chinese Attachments to Calcutta. *Global Networks (Oxford)* 13(2), 220–40.

Blussé, L. (2013). Port Cities of South East Asia, 1400–1800. In P. Clark, ed., *The Oxford Handbook of Cities in World History.* Oxford: Oxford University Press, 346–63.

Booth, A., and K. Deng (2019). Fiscal Development in Taiwan, Korea and Manchuria: Was Japanese Colonialism Different? In E. Frankema and A. Booth, eds., *Fiscal Capacity and the Colonial State in Asia and Africa, c. 1850–1960.* Cambridge: Cambridge University Press, 137–60.

Brenner, N., and C. Schmid (2014). The "Urban Age" in Question. *International Journal of Urban and Regional Research* 38(3), 731–55.

Brown, J. (2012). *City versus Countryside in Mao's China: Negotiating the Divide.* Cambridge: Cambridge University Press.

Calder, K. E. (2016). *Singapore: Smart City, Smart State.* Washington, DC: Brookings Institution Press.

Callahan, W. A. (2013). *China Dreams: Twenty Visions of the Future.* Oxford: Oxford University Press.

Carroll, J. M. (2005). *Edge of Empires: Chinese Elites and British Colonials in Hong Kong.* Cambridge: Harvard University Press.

Cartier, C. (2002). Origins and Evolution of a Geographic Idea: The Macrogregion in China. *Modern China* 28(1), 79–142.

Cartier, C. (2016). A Political Economy of Rank: The Territorial Administrative Hierarchy and Leadership Mobility in Urban China. *Journal of Contemporary China* 25(100), 529–46.

Chaiklin, M. (2012). Introduction. In C. T. van Assendelft de Coningh, *A Pioneer in Yokohama: A Dutchman's Adventures in the New Treaty Port.* M. Chaiklin, ed. and trans. Indianapolis: Hackett, ix–xxvi.

Chalana, M., and T. S. Sprague (2013). Beyond Le Corbusier and the Modernist City: Reframing Chandigarh's "World Heritage" Legacy. *Planning Perspectives* 28(2), 199–222.

Chan, K. W. (2009). The Chinese Hukou System at Fifty. *Eurasian Geography and Economics* 50(2), 197–221.

Chen, J. Y. (2012). *Guilty of Indigence: The Urban Poor in China, 1900–1953.* Princeton: Princeton University Press.

Chen, K.-H., and B. H. Chua, eds. (2007). *The Inter-Asia Cultural Studies Reader.* London: Routledge.

Chen, X. (2014). Steering, Speeding, and Scaling: China's Model of Urban Growth and Its Implications for Cities of the Global South. In S. Parnell and S. Oldfield, eds., *The Routledge Handbook on Cities of the Global South.* London: Taylor & Francis, 155–72.

Chopra, P. (2016). South and South East Asia. In G. Bremner, ed., *Architecture and Urbanism in the British Empire*. Oxford: Oxford University Press. Oxford Scholarship Online. http://doi.org/10.1093/acprof:oso/9780198713326 .001.0001

Chua, B. H. (2017). *Liberalism Disavowed: Communitarianism and State Capitalism in Singapore*. Ithaca: Cornell University Press.

Chua, B. H. (2011). Singapore as Model: Planning Innovations, Knowledge Experts. In A. Roy and A. Ong, eds., *Worlding Cities: Asian Experiments and the Art of Being Global*. Hoboken, NJ: Wiley-Blackwell, 29–54.

Chung, S. (2019). Floating in Mud to Reach the Skies: Victor Sassoon and the Real Estate Boom in Shanghai, 1920s–1930s. *International Journal of Asian Studies* 16(1), 1–31.

Cochran, S. (2000). *Encountering Chinese Networks: Western, Japanese, and Chinese Corporations in China, 1880–1937*. Berkeley: University of California Press.

Cook, J. A. (2011). Reimagining China: Xiamen, Overseas Chinese, and a Transnational Modernity. In M. Y. Dong and J. L. Goldstein, eds., *Everyday Modernity in China*. Seattle: University of Washington Press, 156–94.

Coté, J. (2014). Thomas Karsten's Indonesia. *Bijdragen tot de taal-, land- en volkenkunde* 170(1), 66–98.

Cox, K. R. (2013). Territory, Scale, and Why Capitalism Matters. *Territory, Politics, Governance* 1(1), 46–61.

Datta, P. (2013). How Modern Planning Came to Calcutta. *Planning Perspectives* 28(1), 139–47.

Davidann, J. T. (1998). *A World of Crisis and Progress: The American YMCA in Japan, 1890–1930*. Bethlehem: Lehigh University Press.

Davis, M. (2006). *Planet of Slums*. New York: Verso.

Dawley, E. N. (2019). *Becoming Taiwanese: Ethnogenesis in a Colonial City 1880s–1950s*. Cambridge: Harvard University Asia Center.

de Casparis, J. G., and I. W. Mabbett (1999). Religion and Popular Beliefs in Southeast Asia before c. 1500. In N. Tarling, ed., *The Cambridge History of Southeast Asia*, vol. 1, part 1, *From Early Times to c. 1500*. Cambridge: Cambridge University Press, 276–339.

Dick, H., and P. J. Rimmer (2013). South East Asia and Australia. In P. Clark, ed., *The Oxford Handbook of Cities in World History*. Oxford: Oxford University Press, 580–602.

Dong, M. Y. (2008). Who Is Afraid of the Modern Chinese Girl? In A. E. Weinbaum et al., eds., *The Modern Girl around the World: Consumption, Modernity, and Globalization*. Durham: Duke University Press, 194–219.

Edwards, L. (2020). *Citizens of Beauty: Drawing Democratic Dreams in Republican China*. Seattle: University of Washington Press.

Ericson, S. J. (1996). *The Sound of the Whistle: Railroads and the State in Meiji Japan*. Cambridge: Harvard Asia Center.

Fischer-Tiné, H. (2018). The YMCA and Low-Modernist Rural Development in South Asia, c. 1922–1957. *Past and Present* 240, 193–234.

Fischer-Tiné, H., S. Huebner, and I. Tyrrell (2020). Introduction. In H. Fischer-Tiné, S. Huebner, and I. Tyrrell, eds., *Spreading Protestant Modernity: Global Perspectives on the Social Work of the YMCA and YWCA, 1889–1970*. Honolulu: University of Hawai'i Press, 1–35.

Florida, R. L. (2002). *The Rise of the Creative Class and How It's Transforming Work, Leisure, Community and Everyday Life*. New York: Basic Books.

Fong, A. C. (2014). "Together They Might Make Trouble": Cross-Cultural Interactions in Tang Dynasty Guangzhou, 618–907 C.E. *Journal of World History* 25(4), 475–92.

Gandhi, M. K. (1946). Talk with Press Correspondents. *The Complete Works of Mahatma Gandhi* 84, 226–28.

Gao, J. Z. (2004). *The Communist Takeover of Hangzhou: The Transformation of City and Cadre*. Honolulu: University of Hawai'i Press.

Garon, S. M. (1997). *Molding Japanese Minds: The State in Everyday Life*. Princeton: Princeton University Press.

Gayer, L. (2007). Guns, Slums, and "Yellow Devils": A Genealogy of Urban Conflicts in Karachi, Pakistan. *Modern Asian Studies* 41(3), 515–44.

Gerth, K. (2003). *China Made: Consumer Culture and the Creation of the Nation*. Cambridge: Harvard University Asia Center.

Ghosh, D. (2006). *Sex and the Family in Colonial India: The Making of Empire*. Cambridge: Cambridge University Press.

Ghosh, N. (2020). *A Hygienic City-Nation: Space, Community, and Everyday Life in Colonial Calcutta*. Cambridge: Cambridge University Press.

Gluck, C. (1985). *Japan's Modern Myths: Ideology in the Late Meiji Period*. Princeton: Princeton University Press.

Goebel, M. (2015). *Anti-Imperial Metropolis: Interwar Paris and the Seeds of Third World Nationalism*. New York: Cambridge University Press.

Goodman, B. (2021). *The Suicide of Miss Xi: Democracy and Disenchantment in the Chinese Republic*. Cambridge: Harvard University Press.

Goscha, C. E. (2016). *Vietnam: A New History*. New York: Basic Books.

Grunow, T. R. (2016). Paving Power: Western Urban Planning and Imperial Space from the Streets of Meiji Tokyo to Colonial Seoul. *Journal of Urban History* 42(3), 506–56.

Guha, R., ed. (2011). *Makers of Modern India*. Cambridge: Belknap Press.

Guha, R. (2018). *Gandhi: The Years That Changed the World, 1914–1948*. New York: Knopf.

Haase, D., B. Güneralp, B. Dahiya, X. Bai, and T. Elmqvist (2018). Global Urbanization: Perspectives and Trends. In T. Elmqvist, X. Bai, N. Frantzeskaki, et al., eds., *Urban Planet: Knowledge towards Sustainable Cities*. Cambridge: Cambridge University Press, 19–44.

Hamilton, P. E. (2021). *Made in Hong Kong: Transpacific Networks and a New History of Globalization*. New York: Columbia University Press.

Hammond, K. A. (2020). *China's Muslims and Japan's Empire: Centering Islam in World War II*. Chapel Hill: University of North Carolina Press.

Hanes, J. E. (2002). *The City as Subject: Seki Hajime and the Reinvention of Modern Osaka*. Berkeley: University of California Press.

Hardiman, D. (2003). *Gandhi in His Time and Ours: The Global Legacy of His Ideas*. New York: Columbia University Press.

Harris, R. (2020). The World's First Slum Improvement Programme: Calcutta's Bustees, 1876–1910. *Planning Perspectives* 35(2), 321–44.

Harris, R. (2021). *The Urban Question: How Cities Matter*. Cambridge: Cambridge University Press.

Hausman, W. J., P. Hertner, and M. Wilkins (2008). *Global Electrification: Multinational Enterprise and International Finance in the History of Light and Power, 1878–2007*. Cambridge: Cambridge University Press, 2008.

Havens, T. R. H. (1974). *Farm and Nation in Modern Japan: Agrarian Nationalism, 1870–1940*. Princeton: Princeton University Press.

Hayford, C. W. (1990). *To the People: James Yen and Village China*. New York: Columbia University Press.

Haynes, D. E. (1991). *Rhetoric and Ritual in Colonial India: The Shaping of a Public Culture in Surat City, 1852–1928*. Berkeley: University of California Press.

Headrick, D. R. (1988). *The Tentacles of Progress: Technology Transfer in the Age of Imperialism, 1850–1940*. Oxford: Oxford University Press.

Hein, C. (2003). Visionary Plans and Planners: Japanese Traditions and Western Influences. In N. Fieve and P. Waley, eds., *Japanese Capitals in Historical Perspective: Place, Power and Memory in Kyoto, Edo and Tokyo*. London: Taylor & Francis, 309–46.

Hein, C. (2018). The What, Why, and How of Planning History. In C. Hein, ed., *The Routledge Handbook of Planning History*. New York: Routledge, 1–10.

Heitzman, J. (2008). *The City in South Asia*. London: Routledge.

Hell, S. (2010). *Siam and the League of Nations: Modernisation, Sovereignty and Multilateral Diplomacy 1920–1940*. Bangkok: River Books.

Henry, T. A. (2014). *Assimilating Seoul: Japanese Rule and the Politics of Public Space in Colonial Korea, 1910–1945*. Berkeley: University of California Press.

Hershatter, G. (1997). *Dangerous Pleasures: Prostitution and Modernity in Twentieth-Century Shanghai*. Berkeley: University of California Press.

Hirata, K. (2020). Steel Metropolis: Industrial Manchuria and the Making of Chinese Socialism. *Enterprise and Society* 21(4), 875–85.

Honig, E. (1986). *Sisters and Strangers: Women in the Shanghai Cotton Mills, 1919–1949*. Stanford: Stanford University Press.

Hou, L. (2018). *Building for Oil: Daqing and the Formation of the Chinese Socialist State*. Cambridge: Harvard University Asia Center.

Hsiao, H.-H. M., Y.-F. Hui, and P. Peycam, eds. (2017). *Citizens, Civil Society, and Heritage-Making in Asia*. Singapore: ISEAS.

Huff, G. (2020). *World War II and Southeast Asia: Economy and Society under Japanese Occupation*. Cambridge: Cambridge University Press.

Huffman, J. L. (2018). *Down and Out in Late Meiji Japan*. Honolulu: University of Hawaiʻi Press.

Jasanoff, M. (2005). *Edge of Empire: Lives, Culture, and Conquest in the East, 1750–1850*. New York: Knopf.

Johdka, S. S. (2002). Images of Rural India in Gandhi, Nehru and Ambedkar. *Economic and Political Weekly* 37(32), 3343–53.

Karl, R. E. (2010). *Mao Zedong and China in the Twentieth-Century World: A Concise History*. Durham: Duke University Press.

Keo, B. Z. (2020). Between Empire and Nation(s): The *Peranakan* Chinese of the Straits Settlements, 1890–1948. In M. P. Fitzpatrick and P. Monteith, eds., *Colonialism, China and the Chinese*. New York: Routledge, 99–117.

Kidambi, P. (2007). *The Making of an Indian Metropolis: Colonial Governance and Public Culture in Bombay, 1890–1920*. Aldershot: Ashgate.

Kidambi, P. (2013). South Asia. In P. Clark, ed., *The Oxford Handbook of Cities in World History*. Oxford: Oxford University Press, 561–80.

Kim, C. (2017). Locating Creative City Policy in East Asia: Neoliberalism, Developmental State and Assemblage of East Asian Cities. *International Journal of Cultural Policy* 23(3), 312–30.

Kramer, P. A. (2006). *Blood of Government: Race, Empire, the United States, and the Philippines*. Chapel Hill: University of North Carolina Press.

Kusno, A. (2000). *Behind the Postcolonial: Architecture, Urban Space, and Political Cultures in Indonesia*. New York: Routledge.

Kwak, N. H. (2015). *A World of Homeowners: American Power and the Politics of Housing Aid*. Chicago: University of Chicago Press.

LaCouture, E. (2021). *Dwelling in the World: Family, House, and Home in Tianjin, China, 1860–1960*. New York: Columbia University Press.

Laffan, M. F. (2003). *Islamic Nationhood and Colonial Indonesia: The* Umma *below the Winds*. London: RoutledgeCurzon.

Lee, Y. (1996). *The Ideology of Kokugo: Nationalizing Language in Modern Japan*. M. H. Hubbard, trans. Honolulu: University of Hawai'i Press.

Lees, L. H. (2017). *Planting Empire, Cultivating Subjects: British Malaya, 1786–1941*. Cambridge: Cambridge University Press.

Levine, P. (2004). Sexuality, Gender, and Empire. In P. Levine, ed., *Gender and Empire*. Oxford: Oxford University Press, 134–55.

Lewis, M. W., and K. E. Wigen (1997). *The Myth of Continents: A Critique of Metageography*. Berkeley: University of California Press.

Lewis, S. L. (2016). *Cities in Motion: Urban Life and Cosmopolitanism in Southeast Asia, 1920–1940*. Cambridge: Cambridge University Press.

Lincoln, T. (2021). *An Urban History of China*. Cambridge: Cambridge University Press.

Lowey-Ball, S. (2015). Liquid Market, Solid State: The Rise and Demise of the Great Global Emporium at Malacca, 1400–1641. Ph.D. dissertation, Yale University.

Lu, H. (1999). *Beyond the Neon Lights: Everyday Shanghai in the Early Twentieth Century*. Berkeley: University of California Press.

Maher, M. (2018). Sustainability, Karachi, and Other Irreconcilables. In T. Elmqvist, X. Bai, N. Frantzeskaki, et al., eds., *Urban Planet: Knowledge towards Sustainable Cities*. Cambridge: Cambridge University Press, 353–56.

Mazower, M. (2012). *Governing the World: The History of an Idea, 1815 to the Present*. New York: Penguin Books.

McHale, S. (2004). *Print and Power: Confucianism, Communism, and Buddhism in the Making of Modern Vietnam, 1920–1945*. Honolulu: University of Hawai'i Press.

Merkel-Hess, K. (2016). *The Rural Modern: Reconstructing the Self and State in Republican China*. Chicago: University of Chicago Press.

Mertha, A. C. (2014). *Brothers in Arms: Chinese Aid to the Khmer Rouge, 1975–1979*. Ithaca: Cornell University Press.

Metcalf, T. R. (2007). *Imperial Connections: India in the Indian Ocean Arena, 1860–1920*. Berkeley: University of California Press.

Metcalf, T. R. (2013). Colonial Cities. In P. Clark, ed., *The Oxford Handbook of Cities in World History*. Oxford: Oxford University Press, 753–69.

Meyskens, C. F. (2020). *Mao's Third Front: The Militarization of Cold War China*. Cambridge: Cambridge University Press.

Mishra, P. (2012). *From the Ruins of Empire: The Revolt against the West and the Remaking of Asia*. New York: Picador.

Mitter, R. (2013). *Forgotten Ally: China's World War II, 1937–1945*. Boston: Houghton Mifflin Harcourt.

Mitter, R. (2019). State-Building after Disaster: Jiang Tingfu and the Reconstruction of Post–World War II China, 1943–1949. *Comparative Studies in Society and History*, 61(1), 176–206.

Morley, I. (2018a). *Cities and Nationhood: American Imperialism and Urban Design in the Philippines, 1898–1916*. Honolulu: University of Hawai'i Press.

Morley, I. (2018b). The First Filipino City Beautiful Plans. *Planning Perspectives* 33(3), 433–47.

Morris, J. (2011). *Hong Kong*. New York: Knopf.

Mukherjee, J. (2015). *Hungry Bengal: War, Famine and the End of Empire*. Oxford: Oxford University Press.

Murphey, R. (1980). *The Fading of the Maoist Vision: City and Country in China's Development*. New York: Methuen.

Nasser, Y. A. (2021). Finding "Asia" after Imperialism: Transnational Visions of the "Asian Woman" in India and China, 1949–1955. *Twentieth-Century China* 46(1), 62–68.

Nasution, K. S. (2002). Colonial Intervention and Transformation of Muslim *Waqf* Settlements in Urban Penang: The Role of the Endowments Board. *Journal of Muslim Minority Affairs* 22(2), 299–315.

Nathan, M. A. (2018). *From the Mountains to the Cities: A History of Buddhist Propagation in Modern Korea*. Honolulu: University of Hawai'i Press.

Nightingale, C. H. (2012). *Segregation: A Global History of Divided Cities*. Chicago: University of Chicago Press.

Ong, A. (2011). Introduction: Worlding Cities, or the Art of Being Global. In A. Roy and A. Ong, eds., *Worlding Cities: Asian Experiments and the Art of Being Global*. Malden: Wiley-Blackwell, 1–26.

Padawangi, R., ed. (2019). *Routledge Handbook of Urbanization in Southeast Asia*. London: Taylor & Francis.

Park, A. L. (2014). Reclaiming the Rural: Modern Danish Cooperative Living in Colonial Korea, 1925–37. *Journal of Korean Studies* 19(1), 115–51.

Parnell, S., and S. Oldfield, eds. (2014). *The Routledge Handbook on Cities of the Global South*. London: Taylor & Francis.

Peycam, P. (2013). From the Social to the Political: 1920s Colonial Saigon as a "Space of Possibilities" in Vietnamese Consciousness. *positions: asia critique* 21(3), 496–546.

Pillai, P. (2015). *Yearning to Belong: Malaysia's Indian Muslims, Chitties, Portuguese Eurasians, Peranakan Chinese and Baweanese.* Singapore: ISEAS.

Plomp, M. (2012). The Capital of Pulp Fiction and Other Capitals: Cultural Life in Medan, 1950–1958. In J. Lindsay and M. H. T. Liem, eds., *Heirs to World Culture: Being Indonesian, 1950–1965.* Leiden: KITLV Press, 371–96.

Pomeranz, K. (1993). *The Making of a Hinterland: State, Society, and Economy in Inland North China, 1853–1937.* Berkeley: University of California Press.

Prakash, G., M. Laffan, and N. Menon (2018). Introduction: The Postcolonial Moment. In G. Prakash, M. Laffan, and N. Menon, eds., *The Postcolonial Moment in South and Southeast Asia.* London: Bloomsbury, 1–10.

Rao-Cavale, K. (2017). Patrick Geddes in India: Anti-colonial Nationalism and the Historical Time of "Cities in Evolution." *Landscape and Urban Planning* 166, 71–81.

Ray, A. (2017). *Towns and Cities of Medieval India: A Brief Survey.* New York: Routledge.

Reba, M. L., F. Reitsma, and K. C. Seto (2016). Spatializing 6,000 Years of Global Urbanization from 3700 BC to AD 2000. *Scientific Data* 3, 160034. https://doi.org/10.1038/sdata.2016.34.

Reba, M. L., F. Reitsma, and K. C. Seto (2018). Historical Urban Population: 3700 BC – AD 2000. Palisades: NASA Socioeconomic Data and Applications Center. https://doi.org/10.7927/H4ZG6QBX. Accessed 15 August 2021.

Reid, A. (1999). *Charting the State of Early Modern Southeast Asia.* Chiang Mai: Silkworm.

Reinhardt, A. (2018). *Navigating Semi-colonialism: Shipping, Sovereignty, and Nation-Building in China, 1860–1937.* Cambridge: Harvard University Asia Center.

Remer, C. F. (1933). *Foreign Investments in China.* New York: Macmillan.

Ren, X. (2020). *Governing the Urban in India and China: Land Grabs, Slum Clearance, and the War on Air Pollution.* Princeton: Princeton University Press.

Rimmer, P. (1993). Reshaping Western Pacific Rim Cities: Exporting Japanese Planning Ideas. In Fujita K., and R. Hill, eds., *Japanese Cities in the World Economy.* Philadelphia: Temple University Press, 257–79.

Rodgers, D. T. (1998). *Atlantic Crossings: Social Politics in a Progressive Age.* Cambridge: Harvard University Press.

Rogaski, R. (2004). *Hygienic Modernity: Meanings of Health and Disease in Treaty-Port China.* Berkeley: University of California Press.

Rowe, W. T. (1984). *Hankow: Commerce and Society in a Chinese City, 1796–1889.* Stanford: Stanford University Press.

Rowe, W. T. (2013). China: 1300–1900. In P. Clark, ed., *The Oxford Handbook of Cities in World History*. Oxford: Oxford University Press, 310–27.

Roy, A., and A. Ong, eds. (2011). *Worlding Cities: Asian Experiments and the Art of Being Global*. Hoboken: Wiley-Blackwell.

Sand, J. (2013). *Tokyo Vernacular: Common Spaces, Local Histories, Found Objects*. Berkeley: University of California Press.

Sasaki, M. (2010). Urban Regeneration through Cultural Creativity and Social Inclusion: Rethinking Creative City Theory through a Japanese Case Study. *Cities* 27, supplement 1, S3–S9.

Sassen, S. (1991). *The Global City: New York, London, Tokyo*. Princeton: Princeton University Press.

Saunier, P.-Y., and S. Ewen, eds. (2008). *Another Global City: Historical Explorations into the Transnational Municipal Movement, 1850–2000*. New York: Palgrave Macmillan.

Scott, J. C. (2009). *The Art of Not Being Governed: An Anarchist History of Upland Southeast Asia*. New Haven: Yale University Press.

Seidensticker, E. (1991). *Low City, High City. Tokyo from Edo to the Earthquake: How the Shogun's Ancient Capital became a Great Modern City, 1867–1923*. Cambridge: Harvard University Press.

Sherman, T. C. (2015). *Muslim Belonging in Secular India: Negotiating Citizenship in Postcolonial Hyderabad*. Cambridge: Cambridge University Press.

Shiraishi, T. (2003). A New Regime of Order: The Origin of Modern Surveillance Politics in Indonesia. In J. T. Siegel and A. R. Kahin, eds., *Southeast Asia over Three Generations: Essays Presented to Benedict R. O'G. Anderson*. Ithaca: Cornell Southeast Asia Program, 47–74.

Silver, C. (2008). *Planning the Megacity: Jakarta in the Twentieth Century*. London: Routledge.

Simon, D., and H. Leck (2014). Urban Dynamics and the Challenges of Global Environmental Change in the South. In S. Parnell and S. Oldfield, eds., *The Routledge Handbook on Cities of the Global South*. London: Taylor & Francis, 613–38.

Sinn, E. (2013). *Pacific Crossing: California Gold, Chinese Migration, and the Making of Hong Kong*. Hong Kong: Hong Kong University Press.

Slate, N. (2012). *Colored Cosmopolitanism: The Shared Struggle for Freedom in the United States and India*. Cambridge: Harvard University Press.

Smart, A., and D. Curran (2022). Prospects and Social Impact of Big Data–Driven Urban Governance in China: Provincializing Smart City Research. In W. Wu and Q. Gao, eds., *China Urbanizing: Impacts and Transitions*. Philadelphia: University of Pennsylvania Press, 205–27.

Smith, N. R. (2021). *The End of the Village: Planning the Urbanization of Rural China*. Minneapolis: University of Minnesota Press.

Sorensen, A. (2002). *The Making of Urban Japan: Cities and Planning from Edo to the Twenty-First Century*. London: Taylor & Francis.

Spodek, H. (2011). *Ahmedabad: Shock City of Twentieth-Century India*. Bloomington: Indiana University Press.

Stapleton, K. (2008). Warfare and Modern Urban Administration in Chinese Cities. In S. Cochran and D. Strand, eds., *Cities in Motion: Interior, Coast, and Diaspora in Transnational China*. Berkeley: University of California East Asian Institute, 53–78.

Stapleton, K. (2013). China: 1900 to the Present. In P. Clark, ed., *The Oxford Handbook of Cities in World History*. Oxford: Oxford University Press, 522–41.

Stapleton, K. (2020). Liberation: A View from the Southwest. In A. Baumler, ed., *Routledge Handbook of Revolutionary China*, New York: Routledge, 60–73.

Stapleton, K. (2022). The Rise of Municipal Administration in Early Twentieth-Century China: Local History, International Influence, and National Integration. *Twentieth-Century China* 47(1), 11–19.

Stoler, A. L. (2020). *Carnal Knowledge and Imperial Power: Race and the Intimate in Colonial Rule*. Berkeley: University of California Press.

Subrahmanyam, S. (1993). *The Portuguese Empire in Asia, 1500–1700: A Political and Economic History*. New York: Longman.

Sunar, L. (2019). The Weberian City, Civil Society, and Turkish Social Thought. In E. Hanke, L. Scaff, and S. Whimster, eds., *The Oxford Handbook of Max Weber*. Oxford: Oxford University Press, 207–26.

Tangherlini, T. (2008). Chosŏn Memories: Spectatorship, Ideology, and the Korean Folk Village. In T. Tangherlini and S. Yea, eds., *Sitings: Critical Approaches to Korean Geography*. University of Hawai'i Press, 61–82.

Tam, G. A. (2020). *Dialect and Nationalism in China, 1860–1960*. Cambridge: Cambridge University Press.

Tarling, N. (2001). *A Sudden Rampage: The Japanese Occupation of Southeast Asia, 1941–1945*. Honolulu: University of Hawai'i Press.

Taylor, J. G. (2009). *The Social World of Batavia: Europeans and Eurasians in Colonial Indonesia*. Madison: University of Wisconsin Press.

Thongchai, W. (1994). *Siam Mapped: A History of the Geo-body of a Nation*. Honolulu: University of Hawai'i Press.

Thongchai, W. (2000). The Quest for "Siwilai": A Geographical Discourse of Civilizational Thinking in the Late Nineteenth and Early Twentieth-Century Siam. *Journal of Asian Studies* 59(3), 528–49.

Trocki, C. A. (1990). *Opium and Empire: Chinese Society in Colonial Singapore, 1800–1910*. Ithaca: Cornell University Press.

Trocki, C. A. (1999). Political Structures in the Nineteenth and Early Twentieth Centuries. In N. Tarling, ed., *The Cambridge History of Southeast Asia*, vol. 2, part 1, *From c. 1800 to the 1930s*. Cambridge: Cambridge University Press, 75–126.

Tseng, A. Y. (2018). *Modern Kyoto: Building for Ceremony and Commemoration, 1868–1940*. Honolulu: University of Hawai'i Press.

Tsurumi, E. P. (1990). *Factory Girls: Women in the Thread Mills of Meiji Japan*. Princeton: Princeton University Press.

Tyrrell, I. (2020). Vectors of Practicality: Social Gospel, the North American YMCA in Asia, and the Global Context. In H. Fischer-Tiné, S. Huebner, and I. Tyrrell, eds., *Spreading Protestant Modernity: Global Perspectives on the Social Work of the YMCA and YWCA, 1889–1970*. Honolulu: University of Hawai'i Press, 39–60.

United Nations, Department of Economic and Social Affairs, Population Division (2018). *World Urbanization Prospects: The 2018 Revision*. www .un.org/development/desa/publications/2018-revision-of-world-urbaniza tion-prospects.html.

van der Veer, P. (2014). *The Modern Spirit of Asia: The Spiritual and the Secular in China and India*. Princeton: Princeton University Press.

Vann, M. G. (2007). Building Colonial Whiteness on the Red River: Race, Power, and Urbanism in Paul Doumer's Hanoi, 1897–1902. *Historical Reflections* 33(2), 277–304.

Vlastos, S. (1998). Agrarianism without Tradition: The Radical Critique of Prewar Japanese Modernity. In S. Vlastos, ed., *Mirror of Modernity: Invented Traditions of Modern Japan*. Berkeley: University of California Press, 79–94.

Wakeman, R. (2016). *Practicing Utopia: An Intellectual History of the New Town Movement*. Chicago: University of Chicago Press.

Waley, P. (2013). Japan. In P. Clark, ed., *The Oxford Handbook of Cities in World History*. Oxford: Oxford University Press, 542–60.

Walraven, B. (2000). Religion and the City: Seoul in the Nineteenth Century. *Review of Korean Studies* 3, 178–206.

Wang, Z. (1999). *Women in the Chinese Enlightenment: Oral and Textual Histories*. Berkeley: University of California Press.

Ward, M. M. (2019). *Thought Crime: Ideology and State Power in Interwar Japan*. Durham: Duke University Press.

Watson, J. K. (2011). *The New Asian City: Three-Dimensional Fictions of Space and Urban Form*. Minneapolis: University of Minnesota Press.

Wazir, J. K. (2009). Hafiz Ghulam Sarwar (1873–1954): Philosophies of Islam, Civil Society and Civilizations. In J. K. Wazir, ed., *Straits Muslims: Diasporas of the Northern Passage of the Straits of Malacca*. George Town: Straits G.T., 151–68.

Weinbaum, A. E., L. M. Thomas, P. Ramamurthy, et al., eds. (2008). *The Modern Girl around the World: Consumption, Modernity, and Globalization*. Durham: Duke University Press.

Weinstein, L. (2014). *The Durable Slum: Dharavi and the Right to Stay Put in Globalizing Mumbai*. Minneapolis: University of Minnesota Press.

Westney, D. E. (1987). *Imitation and Innovation: The Transfer of Western Organizational Patterns to Meiji Japan*. Cambridge: Harvard University Press.

Wright, G. (1991). *The Politics of Design in French Colonial Urbanism*. Chicago: University of Chicago Press.

Wu, H. (2005). *Remaking Beijing: Tiananmen Square and the Creation of a Political Space*. Chicago: University of Chicago Press.

Wu, W., and P. Gaubatz (2021). *The Chinese City*. 2nd ed. New York: Routledge.

Xing, J. (1996). *Baptized in the Fire of Revolution: The American Social Gospel and the YMCA in China, 1919–1937*. Bethlehem: Lehigh University Press.

Yang, A. (2003). Indian Convict Workers in Southeast Asia in the Late Eighteenth and Early Nineteenth Centuries. *Journal of World History* 14(2), 179–208.

Yang, D. (2010). *Technology of Empire: Telecommunications and Japanese Expansion in Asia, 1883–1945*. Cambridge: Harvard University Asia Center.

Yang, T. (2019). Redefining Semi-colonialism: A Historiographical Essay on British Colonial Presence in China. *Journal of Colonialism and Colonial History* 20(3).

Ye, X. (2003). *The Dianshizhai Pictorial: Shanghai Urban Life, 1884–1898*. Ann Arbor: Center for Chinese Studies, The University of Michigan.

Yeh, E. T. (2013). *Taming Tibet: Landscape Transformation and the Gift of Chinese Development*. Ithaca: Cornell University Press.

Yeoh, B. S. A. (1996). *Contesting Space: Power Relations and the Urban Built Environment in Colonial Singapore*. Kuala Lumpur: Oxford University Press.

Young, L. (2013). *Beyond the Metropolis: Second Cities and Modern Life in Interwar Japan*. Berkeley: University of California Press.

Zanasi, M. (2013). Western Utopias, Missionary Economics, and the Chinese Village. *Journal of World History* 24(2), 359–87.

Zhang X., and T. Sen (2012). The Chinese in South Asia. In C. Tan, ed., *Routledge Handbook of the Chinese Diaspora*. London: Taylor & Francis, 205–26.

Zhao, H. (2019). China-Japan Compete for Infrastructure Investment in Southeast Asia: Geopolitical Rivalry or Healthy Competition? *Journal of Contemporary China* 28(118), 558–74.

Acknowledgments

I am grateful to my colleagues in the Global Urban History Project, particularly Tracy Neumann and Carl Nightingale, for encouraging me to cross borders and think broadly. Generous comments from Eric Beverley and two anonymous reviewers helped me improve the Element both by seeing its value and by recommending specific changes. Space limitations prevented me from benefiting from all of their thoughtful suggestions. The students in my Fall 2021 "Asian Core" graduate seminar at the University at Buffalo also commented helpfully on the Element and inspired me with their own work. Finally, I'd like to thank all the scholars whose work I cite. Cities are remarkable monuments to collective human effort and so, I find, is urban history.

Cambridge Elements ☰

Global Urban History

Michael Goebel

Graduate Institute Geneva

Michael Goebel is the Pierre du Bois Chair Europe and the World and Associate Professor of International History at the Graduate Institute Geneva. His research focuses on the histories of nationalism, of cities, and of migration. He is the author of Anti-Imperial Metropolis: Interwar Paris and the Seeds of Third World Nationalism (2015).

Tracy Neumann

Wayne State University

Tracy Neumann is an Associate Professor of History at Wayne State University. Her research focuses on global and transnational approaches to cities and the built environment. She is the author of Remaking the Rust Belt: The Postindustrial Transformation of North America (2016) and of essays on urban history and public policy.

Joseph Ben Prestel

Freie Universität Berlin

Joseph Ben Prestel is an Assistant Professor (wissenschaftlicher Mitarbeiter) of history at Freie Universität Berlin. His research focuses on the histories of Europe and the Middle East in the nineteenth and twentieth centuries as well as on global and urban history. He is the author of Emotional Cities: Debates on Urban Change in Berlin and Cairo, 1860–1910 (2017).

About the Series

This series proposes a new understanding of urban history by reinterpreting the history of the world's cities. While urban history has tended to produce single-city case studies, global history has mostly been concerned with the interconnectedness of the world. Combining these two approaches produces a new framework to think about the urban past. The individual titles in the series emphasize global, comparative, and transnational approaches. They deliver empirical research about specific cities, while also exploring questions that expand the narrative outside the immediate locale to give insights into global trends and conceptual debates. Authored by established and emerging scholars whose work represents the most exciting new directions in urban history, this series makes pioneering research accessible to specialists and non-specialists alike.

Cambridge Elements ≡

Global Urban History

Elements in the Series

A full series listing is available at: www.cambridge.org/EGUB

Printed in the United States
by Baker & Taylor Publisher Services